Valentina's
ITALIAN FAMILY FEAST

Valentina's
ITALIAN FAMILY FEAST

VALENTINA HARRIS

Special photography by
Jacqui Hurst

SIMON & SCHUSTER
New York   London   Toronto   Sydney   Tokyo   Singapore

For B.J.W. – one of life's great givers

SIMON & SCHUSTER
Simon & Schuster Building
Rockefeller Center
1230 Avenue of the Americas
New York, New York 10020

SIMON & SCHUSTER and colophon are registered trademarks
of Simon & Schuster Inc.

First published in Great Britain in 1990
by Conran Octopus Limited
37 Shelton Street
London WC2H 9HN

Art Director	Mary Evans
Art Editor	Peter Cross
Editor	Denise Bates
American Editor	Norma MacMillan
Picture Research	Nadine Bazar
Production	Sonya Sibbons
Italian Photographic Co-ordinator	Ian Rooks
Home Economist	Valerie Barrett

Typeset by Litho Link Limited, Welshpool, Powys, Wales
Printed in Hong Kong

1   3   5   7   9   10   8   6   4   2

ISBN 0-671-74530-1

Library of Congress Cataloging in Publication Data Available

CONTENTS

INTRODUCTION

This is the book about Italian food that I have always wanted to write. The idea behind it was to give the reader an insight into what Italian food is *really* about – celebration! And there seemed no better way to show how rooted Italian cooking is in the simple enjoyment of good food in good company than with my own family and friends.

In the course of collecting these authentic recipes Jacqui, the photographer, and I traveled the length and breadth of Italy, calling in on friends and relatives and inviting ourselves to special and everyday occasions alike. The book is completely different from anything else I have written, because it is concerned with absolute spontaneity. The photographs and recipes are what was actually cooked and eaten on the day itself; there is not a single studio picture anywhere.

The sections of the book are divided into menus which give a very good idea of how to combine the various flavors and textures. It

is just these combinations which can make beautifully simple Italian food also delightfully complex and this is one of the principles I set out to put across in the chapters which follow.

There were so many willing friends who became involved in the putting together of this book – to all of them, I would like to express my deepest thanks. In particular, I would like to thank Ferruccio Nobile Migliore for all the shopping and preparation, Leonora Carpi for her contacts and Maurizio for entertaining us so well in Perugia. I would also like to say a very big thank you to the Gelmetti family in Lodi for helping me out again and feel I should apologize for waking them so early on a Sunday morning! My thanks and affection also go to Eleonora Consoli, and to Katia Fongoli. It is wonderful to be reminded that the spirit of hospitality and the joy of sharing are still alive and well in Italian families. Last, but by no means least, thank you to Ian and Edward.

RUSTIC TABLE (right) *Tree trunks provide the legs for this laden table on a farm in Sicily.*

ROME IN THE RAIN (right) *Customers are rather sparse at these market stalls in central Rome.*

IL VENERDÌ SANTO

Good Friday

When I was a little girl growing up in Italy, eating meat on Fridays was absolutely *never* done. Fridays were always taken up with trips to the fish stall and the subsequent preparation of whatever fish looked freshest. Only very rough seas could prevent the fishermen from supplying Friday's meal – in this case we had to eat dried salt cod or stockfish. Although I have come to appreciate the flavor of dried fish, at seven it was rather hard to stomach.

Later on the Pope changed all that. I know a few very religious Catholics who still persist in eating only fish on a Friday, but for almost everyone else things have relaxed considerably. Good Friday, however, is still the day when meat is never served and fish is the central part of the meal.

This is not a day for celebration – it is a somber occasion in Italy, with the church bells tolling steadily in the villages. However,

FISH SHOP (right) *Once a day of fasting and abstinence, Good Friday is still the day when fish, and never meat, is traditionally eaten.*

as it is a national holiday, many families find themselves gathered together and so despite the seriousness of the day, there *is* a hint of enjoyment in the air.

As we were in Rome for Easter, I very much wanted to eat the traditional Roman *frittata del Venerdì Santo*, which is a lettuce omelette flavored with sweet wine. I know it sounds odd, but it is in fact delicious, and, like so many other traditional recipes, in danger of disappearing. Ferruccio made his superb *ravioli di pesce* and served the clear soup in which the fish had been poached as a very light appetizer. This may not sound to everyone's taste, but in fact the soup is a marvelous way to begin the meal – it's known as an *apristomaco*, or stomach opener! For the ravioli he used the most deliciously fine dough.

As a main course, Ferruccio had chosen two different types of fish from his favorite and trusted mar-

FERRUCIO'S DINING ROOM (right) *Our Good Friday lunch in Rome had a suitably splendid setting in Ferrucio's apartment.*

ket stall. We had fillets of sole cooked with butter and oranges and then a much more dramatic and imposing fish baked in the oven with olives. Leonora had bought mounds of purple-headed artichokes and brilliant, emerald-green fresh peas to serve as the main vegetable with the fish.

Dessert was in the form of *la pastiera*, an amazing cake whose origins date back to Ancient Rome. It was first prepared at this time of year to celebrate spring-time and fertility, which explains why it is made with wheat grain! Over the centuries, the Neapoli-tans have adopted it as their traditional Easter cake and nowa-days it can be bought in *pasticcerie* at Easter time. However, I can assure you that the *pastiera* you buy in Naples is completely diffe-rent from any version of the cake made elsewhere. The one we ate was homemade and very special, but there is a small Neapolitan pastry shop near the Opera House in Rome which makes them almost as well. If you do make the cake at home, make sure the grain has been soaked very thoroughly, and do remember to change the water frequently during the days the grain is soaking to prevent it from sprouting.

Menu

Brodo di Pesce

Ravioli di Pesce

Frittata del Venerdì Santo

Orata alle Olive

Carciofi e Pisellini alla Romana

Filetti di Sogliola all'Arancia

La Pastiera

BRODO DI PESCE

Fish Broth

SERVES *6*

2¼ *lb assorted fish, among which there should be
some of the following: red mullet (goatfish), gray
mullet, sea bass, cod, and hake*
1 small onion, quartered
2 stalks celery, quartered
3 sprigs of fresh parsley
2 sprigs of fresh rosemary
1 small lemon, sliced
salt
2 wineglasses of dry white wine

Clean and wash the various fish or pieces of
fish. Lay them in a fairly deep saucepan and
put the vegetables, herbs, and lemon on top.
Sprinkle generously with salt and pour in the
wine. Cover sparingly with water and bring to
a boil. Simmer, covered, about 40 minutes to 1
hour. Remove from the heat and take the fish
out of the broth.

To make a thick soup, take all the flesh off
the fish and purée it in a vegetable mill or food
processor, then stir it back into the broth.

For clear fish broth, strain the liquid
carefully, discarding the vegetables, herbs, and
lemon, and heat to just below boiling. The fish
can be used in another recipe, for example the
one following.

You can also use the broth to make delicious
fish risotto, or add it to fishy pasta sauces. Or
boil tiny pasta in the broth to make a
nourishing and simple soup.

FRESH FISH *Ferruccio invariably buys fish at a local
market stall he knows he can rely on.*

RAVIOLI DI PESCE

Fish Ravioli

SERVES 6

Pasta
3½ cups all-purpose flour
5 extra large eggs
a pinch of salt
½ teaspoon olive oil
Filling
⅔ of the fish from brodo di pesce (see p. 10)
⅓ cup ricotta cheese
2 tablespoons chopped fresh parsley
a pinch of grated nutmeg
salt and freshly ground pepper
Dressing
5 tablespoons unsalted butter, melted but not browned

Make the pasta first: sift the flour onto the work top, make a hole in the center with your fist, and put the eggs into the hole. Add the salt and oil and blend everything together with your fingertips. Knead together very thoroughly until you have a ball of smooth, elastic dough. Begin to roll it out, then fold it in half and roll it out again. Continue to do this until you hear the air pop out from the fold as you press down with the rolling pin. At this point the dough is ready to fill.

Roll it out one last time, as thinly as possible, and cut it all into rounds of about 2½ inches in diameter with a cookie cutter or overturned glass. Leave the rounds on the work top while you quickly make the filling. (Don't leave them too long or they'll dry out and won't seal properly.)

Mash or purée the flesh from the fish and

After cutting out the pasta rounds, fill and seal them quickly so that they do not dry out.

RAVIOLI DI PESCE (left), BRODO DI PESCE (right)

mix it with all the other filling ingredients. Arrange small teaspoonfuls in the center of each pasta round. Fold the rounds in half and press them tightly closed with the tines of a fork, making little grooves along the edge.

Toss the ravioli into a large pot of boiling salted water and cook them about 2 or 3 minutes. Scoop them out carefully with a slotted spoon then cover with the melted butter and serve.

FRITTATA DEL VENERDÌ SANTO

Good Friday Omelette

SERVES 6–8

7 tablespoons olive oil
2 onions, chopped
1 head of romaine lettuce, trimmed, washed and finely chopped
a handful of arugula, washed and chopped
3 tablespoons vin santo or other sweet wine
salt and freshly ground pepper
10 eggs, beaten
5 tablespoons freshly grated Parmesan cheese, or 3 tablespoons Parmesan and 2 tablespoons freshly grated Romano cheese

Heat half the oil in a wide pan, and put all the vegetables into the oil. Cook until soft over a medium heat, turning frequently. Add the wine and boil to evaporate the fumes 2–3 minutes, then season with plenty of salt and freshly ground pepper.

Beat the eggs with the cheese and season with salt and pepper. Heat the remaining oil in a large skillet until sizzling. Mix the vegetables into the egg and cheese mixture, then quickly tip this into the hot oil. Spread out in an even layer and cook until set and golden brown on the bottom, shaking the pan frequently to prevent the omelette from sticking too much.

If using a non-stick pan, turn the omelette out onto a big plate or lid, then slide it back into the pan the other way up. Cook the other side until well browned. Otherwise, leave the omelette in the pan and cook the top under a hot broiler. Serve hot or cold.

ORATA ALLE OLIVE

Baked Fish with Olives

SERVES 6

1 or 2 whole gilt-head bream, porgy or red snapper,
total weight about 4½ lb, drawn
½ cup olive oil
½ cup green olives, pitted
1 cup black olives, pitted
4 cloves garlic, coarsely chopped
4 bay leaves, coarsely chopped
4 sprigs of fresh rosemary, coarsely chopped
salt

Wash and dry the fish thoroughly. Pull the spine away from the flesh as much as possible by inserting the point of a knife under the bone and pulling outward. Fill the fish and cover it with the olives. Sprinkle the garlic, bay leaves, rosemary, and salt over and inside the fish. Place in an oiled baking dish and drizzle the oil over the fish.

Place the dish in a baking pan containing enough water to come halfway up the sides of the dish. Bake in a preheated moderate oven (350°F) about 35 minutes or until the fish will flake easily when it is tested with a skewer. Serve hot.

OLIVES AND SPRIGS OF ROSEMARY *The flavor of fresh rosemary blends beautifully with olives.*

CARCIOFI E PISELLINI ALLA ROMANA

Roman Artichokes with Peas

SERVES 6

6 large globe artichokes
1 large lemon, quartered
1 large onion, chopped
4 slices of prosciutto crudo, very finely chopped
5 tablespoons olive oil
3 sprigs of fresh mint, finely chopped
3 cloves garlic, chopped
salt and freshly ground pepper
2 cups shelled fresh peas

Cut all the outside layers off the artichokes and trim off sharp points. Cut the artichokes in half and remove the furry choke. Soak in a bowl of cold water with the lemon quarters about 30 minutes.

Put the onion and prosciutto into a deep, wide skillet and begin to fry gently together. Add the oil, mint, and garlic and cook a further 5 minutes.

Drain the artichokes and add them to the pan. Season. Cover and cook about 15 minutes, occasionally pouring a little water over the artichokes to prevent them drying out and stirring from time to time. When they are fairly tender, add the peas and cook a further 10 minutes or until both vegetables are completely tender. Serve hot or cold.

FILETTI DI SOGLIOLA ALL'ARANCIA

Fillets of Sole with Orange

SERVES 6–8

5 tablespoons unsalted butter
12 fillets of sole or flounder
grated rind and juice of 1 orange
salt

Melt the butter in 2 wide skillets and cook the fillets of sole gently in the butter for 2 minutes on each side. Reserve the juices and put the fish on a dish to keep warm.

Combine the fish juices in one pan and add the orange juice, grated rind and seasoning. Heat, pour all over the fish and serve.

CARCIOFI E PISELLINI ALLA ROMANA

FILETTI DI SOGLIOLA ALL'ARANCIA

LA PASTIERA

Traditional Neapolitan Easter Cake

For this recipe you need wheat which has been soaked in cold water for about 8 days.

MAKES ONE 12-INCH CAKE

Filling
approx 1 cup dried wheat berries
2 cups milk
pared rind of ½ lemon
2 large pinches of ground cinnamon
1 cup sugar
2 teaspoons vanilla extract
1 lb (2 cups) freshest possible ricotta cheese
grated rind of ½ lemon
3 tablespoons orange flower water
½ cup very finely chopped candied
orange and lime peel
6 egg yolks
4 egg whites

Pastry
2 cups all-purpose flour
5 oz (⅔ cup) freshest possible lard
¾ cup sugar
3 egg yolks

To Finish
lard for greasing
1 egg, beaten
confectioners' sugar for dusting

Soak the wheat in cold water 8 days in a cool place. Change the water at least once a day during this time. At the end of the 8 days, drain and rinse the grain very thoroughly. Weigh out 9 ounces and discard the rest.

LA PASTIERA

Put the weighed grain in a saucepan. Bring the milk to a boil in another pan, then pour it all over the grain. Add the pared lemon rind, a pinch of cinnamon and a heaped tablespoon of the sugar. Stir well. Simmer about 2 hours on the lowest possible heat.

While the grain cooks, make the pastry. Sift the flour onto the work top in a pile, make a hole in the center, and put the lard, sugar, and egg yolks into the hole. Blend all these ingredients together very quickly with your fingertips (or in a food processor) to make a smooth dough. Do not knead the dough: work it only for the time it takes to make an amalgamated mass. Wrap the ball of dough and rest in the refrigerator about 30 minutes.

When the grain has absorbed all the liquid and is just falling apart, take it off the heat and leave to cool completely in the covered pan.

Rub the ricotta through a sieve into a bowl and add the rest of the sugar, cinnamon, the grated lemon rind, orange flower water and candied fruit. Mix together lightly, then add the egg yolks *one at a time*, making sure each one is well blended in before you add another. Beat the egg whites until stiff. Stir the cooled grain, then fold in the egg whites.

Grease a deep 12-inch cake pan generously with lard. Roll out about two-thirds of the pastry dough and use to line the pan. Pour the ricotta filling into the center and smooth it out carefully. Roll out the remaining pastry dough and cut into strips. Use to make a lattice pattern on the filling, anchoring the strips securely to the edges of the pastry case. Brush the pastry with beaten egg. Bake in a pre-heated oven, (350°F) 1 hour or until golden brown and firm to the touch. Let the cake cool in the pan, then sprinkle it generously with sifted confectioners' sugar. The cake is better eaten a few days after baking.

LA PASQUA

Easter Sunday

As a complete contrast to Good Friday, Easter Sunday really is about celebrating. The most devout will have been to church at midnight on Saturday, so the whole of Sunday can be given over to being with one's family and to the sheer indulgent enjoyment of the main feast.

Everybody always has lamb (or kid) on Easter Sunday in Italy, cooked in many different ways. In some households it is cooked over an open fire on a spit or very large grill, while others will braise it with vegetables or make some kind of stew. Whatever is done with it, for many families in the north of Italy this is the only day of the year when lamb is eaten – although of course this doesn't apply to the south, where it is virtually the only meat that is widely cooked.

For anybody who still had room after the main courses, we had the traditional savory *torta pasqualina* – the Ligurian Easter cake made with 33 layers, one for each year of Christ's life, and finally a *colomba,* the dove-shaped Easter cake that is sold all over Italy but which can also be made at home if you feel so inclined. When I was a child you could only buy the plain kind with almond

and sugar topping, but nowadays they come with all kinds of fillings and icings and frostings, from champagne mousse to strawberry gelatin. Take a tip from me, however – the old-fashioned one is by far the nicest!

When everybody was absolutely full up, it was time to allow the children to dive into the colorfully wrapped chocolate Easter eggs, in which a present,

usually a toy, is hidden. The egg hunt then took over for the rest of the afternoon. My mother hides painted eggs for her grandchildren, just as she always hid them for us when we were young, and there seemed to be such a lot of eggs, hidden on the handlebars of bicycles, in the forks of trees, under lettuce in the vegetable garden and in a thousand and one other places which are used year after year. There have to be lots of eggs, otherwise the whole thing would be over in minutes! As nobody ever bothers to count how many eggs have been hidden, the hunt is over when no more can be found. The funny thing is, we then spend the following few weeks discovering more eggs hidden all over the garden . . .

Menu

Lasagnette con Spinaci e Funghi

Agnello Braciato

Fave in Purè

Patate Arrosto

Carote al Latte

La Torta Pasqualina

La Colomba

EASTER EGGS (left) *Hidden inside each lavishly wrapped chocolate egg is a present, usually a toy.*

OPENING THE EGGS (left) *With my excited children the usual result is a lot of broken chocolate!*

LASAGNETTE CON SPINACI E FUNGHI

Lasagnette with Spinach and Mushrooms

SERVES 6

1 lb fresh bulk spinach
10 tablespoons (1¼ sticks) butter
salt and freshly ground pepper
1 oz dried funghi porcini, *soaked in warm water*
10 minutes and rinsed well
1 lb lasagnette or mafalda
½ cup cream
⅔ cup freshly grated Parmesan cheese

Wash the spinach, then cook it in 2 or 3 tablespoons of water until it is just soft. Squeeze it dry with your hands, then chop it finely with a sharp knife. Put the spinach in a pan with half the butter and sauté it briefly just 2 or 3 minutes.

Bring a large pot of salted water to a boil. Drain the mushrooms, chop them finely, and add them to the spinach. Mix the spinach and mushrooms together over a low heat. Season to taste. Remove from the heat and keep the vegetables warm.

When the water boils, toss in the lasagnette or mafalda and boil until *al dente* (check package for timing as brands vary).

Drain the pasta and tip it into a warmed bowl. Add the warm spinach and mushroom mixture, the rest of the butter, and the cream. Toss everything together very thoroughly and season well.

Sprinkle with the Parmesan and toss once more before serving.

AGNELLO BRACIATO

Braised Lamb

SERVES 6

6 tablespoons butter
4 tablespoons sunflower oil
1 leg of lamb, boned weight about 4½ lb
1 large onion, thickly sliced
1 large carrot, coarsely chopped
2 large stalks celery, coarsely chopped
a handful of fresh parsley, coarsely chopped
salt and freshly ground pepper
2 large wineglasses of dry white wine
2 cups broth or stock

Heat half the butter with the oil in a deep flameproof casserole for 2 or 3 minutes, then seal the leg of lamb all over in the hot fat, browning it well. Remove the lamb and wrap in foil to keep warm. Put all the vegetables and the parsley into the casserole and cook gently until soft and golden brown. Add a little water if they begin to get too brown or stick to the casserole. When the vegetables are cooked, return the meat to the casserole with any juices which have leaked out into the foil. Season.

Add a little wine, and boil to evaporate the fumes 3 minutes. Continue in this way until all the wine has been added. Add the broth or stock a little at a time, turning the meat each time and allowing the liquid to evaporate before you add any more. This takes about 1½ hours – make sure you keep the heat low and let the meat cook slowly.

When the meat is ready, it will be well browned and coated in a glossy brown sauce. Remove the meat from the casserole and slice it carefully. Arrange the slices on a warm platter. Add a little more wine or stock to the sauce in the casserole and bring it to a boil, stirring. Add the rest of the butter and stir until melted, then pour this sauce over the sliced meat. Serve at once.

LAMB ON A SPIT (left) *Some families roast their Easter lamb on a spit over the open fire.*

FAVE IN PURÈ

Purée of Fava Beans

SERVES 6

3¼ lb fresh fava beans in their pods, or frozen lima beans
salt and freshly ground pepper
⅔ cup cream
1 stick of butter
1 teaspoon sugar

Shell the fava beans and remove their tough inner skins. This may seem time-consuming but it really enhances the taste. Rinse them carefully. Cook in boiling salted water about 5 minutes (frozen beans need about 12 minutes). Drain the beans and push them through a vegetable mill or whizz in a food processor to make a smooth purée.

Return the purée to the saucepan and heat gently, stirring constantly. Add the cream a little at a time, still stirring, then add the butter and sugar. Finally, season to taste with salt and freshly ground pepper, and serve the purée piping hot.

(left to right) CAROTE AL LATTE, PATATE ARROSTO, AGNELLO BRACIATO

PATATE ARROSTO

Roast Potatoes

SERVES 6

1¼ lb potatoes suitable for roasting
⅔ cup sunflower oil
3 cloves garlic
salt and freshly ground pepper

Peel the potatoes and cut them into equal-sized 1½-inch chunks. Part-cook them in boiling salted water 2–3 minutes, then drain. Heat the oil with the peeled garlic in a baking pan in a preheated moderately hot oven (400°F) until the garlic turns golden brown. Remove the baking pan from the oven and add the potatoes. Season generously and turn the potatoes so they are coated all over with the garlic-flavored oil. Spread the potatoes out evenly in the pan.

Return to the oven to roast until crisp and golden brown. This should take about 45 minutes. Serve very hot.

LEAVING CHURCH ON SUNDAY MORNING *It is a tradition on Easter Sunday morning to take food to the church to be blessed.*

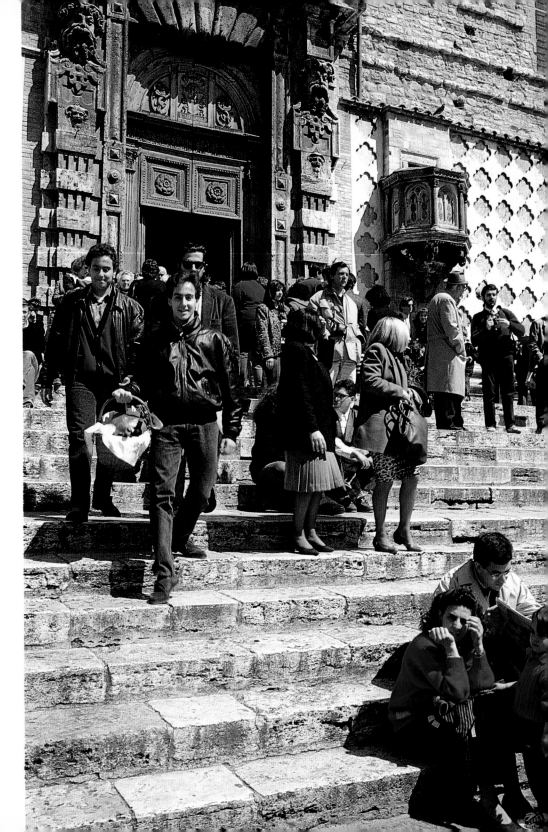

CAROTE AL LATTE

Carrots in Milk

SERVES 6

1½ lb carrots, sliced into rounds
salt and freshly ground pepper
1 tablespoon butter
1 cup milk
1 egg yolk

Bring a saucepan of salted water to a boil, toss in the carrots and cook 5 minutes. Drain the carrots and put them in a large pan with the butter and three-quarters of the milk. Season to taste. Cook a further 6 or 7 minutes, or until tender. Season well. Add the rest of the milk and the egg yolk and stir quickly together to thicken the sauce. Watch the sauce carefully and as soon as it thickens transfer everything to a warmed dish and serve immediately.

LA TORTA PASQUALINA

Ligurian Easter Pie

SERVES 10–12

2¼ lb frozen filo pastry, thawed (you will need 18-33 sheets, large enough to cover the bottom of a 12-inch cake pan)
12 globe artichokes, as young and tender as possible
1 onion, finely sliced
juice of 1 lemon
6 tablespoons olive oil
salt and freshly ground pepper
4 slices of stale white bread, crusts removed
⅔ cup milk
10 eggs, as fresh as possible
8 heaped tablespoons freshly grated Parmesan cheese
1¼ lb (2½ cups) ricotta or whipped cream cheese
melted butter or oil for brushing pastry
1 stick of unsalted butter, finely diced
1 tablespoon chopped fresh marjoram

Prepare the artichokes (see p.13). Cut each artichoke in half, remove the choke with a teaspoon, and slice the artichoke. Put the slices

LA TORTA PASQUALINA (right)

in a saucepan immediately with the onion, lemon juice, and about 5 tablespoons of olive oil. Cook gently about 20 minutes, stirring frequently. Season with salt and pepper.

While the artichokes are cooking, soak the bread 10 minutes in the milk, in a large bowl. In another bowl, beat 4 eggs with 3 tablespoons of the grated Parmesan. Stir this mixture into the bread and milk. Add the cooked artichokes, then the ricotta. Mix very thoroughly, then set to one side until required.

Oil a 12-inch cake pan, which needs to be fairly deep, preferably about 5 inches. Lay the first sheet of pastry on the bottom of the cake pan and brush it with butter. Continue to layer the sheets in the pan, brushing each one with butter before you put in the next one. On the 11th sheet, spread the artichoke filling. Using the back of a spoon, make 6 little hollows in the surface of the filling. Put a tiny piece of unsalted butter in each hollow, then break an egg on top of the butter, being very careful not to break the yolk. Cover each egg with grated Parmesan, and sprinkle with salt, pepper, and marjoram. Lay the next sheet of pastry over the filling, brush it with butter, and dot a little unsalted butter all around the edge. Lay in another sheet, brush it with butter, and dot unsalted butter around the edges. Continue in this way until you have used up all the pastry. Any pastry which hangs over the edge of the pan must be folded back and pressed down lightly to create a thicker band around the edge of the pie. When cooked it will give you a very crisp crust.

Pierce holes with a skewer all over the surface of the pie, then brush very thoroughly with butter. Place in a preheated moderately hot oven (375°F) and bake 1 hour. Serve warm or cold, as part of a buffet or for a special occasion picnic.

LA COLOMBA

Easter Dove Cake

MAKES ONE 10–INCH CAKE

8 cups all-purpose flour
¾ oz active dry yeast
8 egg yolks
a pinch of salt
grated rind of 1 lemon
14 oz (3½ sticks) unsalted butter
1½ cups sugar
½ cup milk
2 cups chopped mixed candied fruit
⅔ cup golden raisins
1 egg, beaten
2–3 tablespoons crushed rock candy

Set aside about 1⅓ cups of flour, for dusting the work surface and flouring your hands.

Pour 2 quarts of water into a deep saucepan and warm until just lukewarm. Pour about 4 tablespoons of the lukewarm water into a large bowl, sprinkle in the yeast and blend together. Mix in ¾ cup of the flour, making a dry, firm dough. Roll this into a ball. Drop this ball into the lukewarm water and leave it there 10 minutes, at which point it should rise up to the surface. Turn it over and leave it floating for about 15 minutes, turning it over occasionally.

Meanwhile, put the remaining flour, minus the quantity set aside, into a very large mixing bowl (3 times the size of the ball of dough). Add to it the 8 egg yolks, the pinch of salt, grated lemon rind, about half of the butter, the sugar, the milk and the ball of dough which has been floating in water. Flour your hands and knead all this very thoroughly. If necessary, add a little more milk and flour from the quantity set aside and work at the dough until it is no longer sticky.

When it is completely smooth and elastic, put the dough into a bowl and place it in a warm place (about 77°F) to rise. (Beware of drafts.) When it has risen by one third, take it out and punch it down, then add about half of the remaining butter. Knead thoroughly, working in more flour if necessary, then return to the bowl in the warm place. When it has again risen by one third, punch it down and add the remaining butter (saving enough for greasing), the candied fruit and raisins.

Butter a deep 10-inch cake pan, then put in the dough. Cover with wax paper and allow the dough to rise 30 minutes. Then remove the paper and brush the surface with egg and sprinkle with rock candy. Let the dough rest 5 minutes, then bake in a preheated moderately hot oven (375°F) 10 minutes. Lower the heat to (350°F) and cover the cake with brown paper or foil to prevent it browning too much. Bake 1-1¼ hours or until a wooden toothpick inserted into the cake comes out clean. Cool on a wire rack.

PAINTED EGGS (above) *for the egg hunt.*
LA COLOMBA (right)

ALEMAGNA

UN PRANZO MOLTO RUSTICO

A Rustic Lunch

Probably the most vital aspect of all Italian cuisine is *la cucina povera*, the peasant cuisine from which so much of Italian cooking sprang. This is food made with ingredients and following recipes which have changed very little over the centuries, despite the changes in Italy's economy. By and large, it aims at filling stomachs while being as tasty and nourishing as possible, and because it was born out of necessity and local availability, there are absolutely no rigid rules – you can adapt and add your own touches as you like.

Probably the most enduring combination is that of pasta with the simplest of tomato sauces. Particularly in the south, large periods of time during August and September are dedicated to bottling fresh tomato sauce for the winter months. When I was a child we used to do this out in the garden: all those who had been enlisted for the job crouched around an old tin bath placed over

an open fire, with the bottles of tomatoes, wrapped tightly in newspaper, being boiled in the bath. It was incredibly hot work, and the mountains of overripe tomatoes never appeared to get any smaller. It seemed incredibly cruel sometimes, to be stuck at home doing this when the late summer sea with its great foaming waves was beckoning. But in February, when the rain was horizontal and the damp inescapable, it was just like having sunshine on your plate when the bottles were opened and the fragrant sauces poured out.

Menu

Minestra di Pasta e Broccoli

Pezzelle di Pane

Cappuccio Imbottito

Maltagliati al Sugo di Pomodoro

Rognone di Vitello alla Furnacella

Albanesi

MALTAGLIATI AL SUGO DI POMODORO (right), *eaten directly from the traditional wooden trough.*

RUSTIC STOREHOUSE (right) *These traditional utensils have changed little over the centuries.*

MINESTRA DI PASTA E BROCCOLI

Broccoli and Pasta Soup

SERVES 6

¼ lb bacon fat, lard or ham fat
2 cloves garlic, finely chopped
½ dried small red chili pepper
1 bunch of light green broccoli, weighing about 5 oz
cut into very small florets
½ cup dry white wine
3 cups cold water
salt and freshly ground pepper
¾ lb cannolicchietti or tiny Ave Marie
(very small pasta suitable for soups)
freshly grated Romano cheese to taste

Fry the fat with the garlic and chili until golden brown and sizzling. Add the broccoli and wine and cook about 3 minutes, then add the water and cover the pan. Simmer about 12 minutes or until the broccoli is tender, adding more water as required. Season with plenty of salt and pepper.

As soon as the broccoli is cooked, tip in the pasta and cook until it is *al dente*. Add plenty of freshly grated Romano cheese to taste and serve hot, warm or cold.

BOTTLED VEGETABLES (right) *Abundant summer vegetables are preserved and eaten as antipasti during the sparser winter months.*

PEZZELLE DI PANE

Baked Dry Bread with Cheese

SERVES 4–6

4 thick slices of stale Italian bread, as coarse as possible
1¼ cups milk
6 tablespoons olive oil
1 clove garlic, minced
5 canned tomatoes, chopped
a large pinch of dried oregano
salt and freshly ground pepper
1 lb scamorza cheese (dried mozzarella) or fresh mozzarella cheese

Place the bread on a plate and cover with the milk. When it is wet through, arrange the bread on the bottom of an ovenproof dish, making sure it is tightly packed together.

Fry the oil, garlic, and tomatoes together in a saucepan about 15 minutes. Season with the oregano, and salt and pepper to taste, then pour the tomato mixture over the bread. Arrange the sliced cheese on top. Bake in a preheated moderately hot oven (400°F) about 15 minutes.

THE LUNCH TABLE (right) *Plates are superfluous with this wooden trough into which the pasta is piled; everyone around the table then simply helps themselves.*

CAPPUCCIO IMBOTTITO

Stuffed Cabbage Leaves

SERVES 6

2–3 tablespoons olive oil
1 large onion, chopped
1 lb ground meat (beef, lamb, veal, chicken, etc.)
⅔ cup dry white wine
1 quart puréed tomatoes
about 12 large cabbage leaves
¾ cup long-grain rice
freshly grated Romano cheese, to taste
salt and freshly ground pepper

Heat the oil in a pan and fry the onion about 6 minutes. Add the meat and brown it carefully all over. Add the wine and allow to evaporate about 3 minutes, then add the puréed tomatoes and stir. Cover the pan and simmer the sauce 20–30 minutes.

Meanwhile, bring a large pot of water to a boil and cook the cabbage leaves 10–12 minutes or until they are just soft. Drain and leave to cool.

Cook the rice in boiling salted water until just tender; drain.

Fill each cabbage leaf with about 1 table-spoonful of rice until all the rice is used up.

Pour some of the sauce over the bottom of an ovenproof dish and sprinkle the sauce with grated Romano. Arrange the filled cabbage leaves on top and cover with the rest of the sauce and cheese. Bake in a preheated moderately hot oven (400°F) about 15 minutes or until heated through. Serve hot or cold.

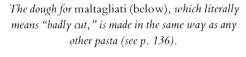

The dough for maltagliati (below), *which literally means "badly cut," is made in the same way as any other pasta (see p. 136).*

When the dough has been rolled out, fold it into three and make rough, irregular cuts across it (bottom left). When all the dough has been cut, open out the strips and scatter them over a floured work top.

Leave the strips to dry out a little about 10–20 minutes, then gather them together to use (below center).

MALTAGLIATI AL SUGO DI POMODORO (below)

MALTAGLIATI AL SUGO DI POMODORO

Maltagliati with Tomato Sauce

SERVES 6

5 tablespoons olive oil
1 onion, finely chopped
1 large stalk celery, finely chopped
1 carrot, finely chopped
1 quart passata *(tomato purée)*
salt and freshly ground pepper
1¼ lb maltagliati *or other pasta of your choice*
To finish
a handful of fresh basil, arugula or cilantro leaves,
torn into strips with your fingers
freshly grated Parmesan or Romano cheese to taste

Heat the oil in a saucepan and fry the onion, celery, and carrot about 3–5 minutes, then add the *passata* and season to taste. Simmer covered about 30 minutes. Remove from the heat and let the sauce stand, covered, until required.

Bring a large pot of salted water to a boil. Toss in the pasta and cook until *al dente* (check package for cooking time as brands vary). Drain the pasta and return to the pan. Pour the sauce over, toss together thoroughly, and scatter the herb of your choice over the top. (I do not recommend a combination of these or any other herbs; choose one and stick to it.) Sprinkle generously with freshly grated Parmesan or Romano and serve.

MALTAGLIATI *are left to dry out in the fresh air before use* (right).

ROGNONE DI VITELLO ALLA FURNACELLA

Grilled Lamb Kidneys

Although the original recipe uses kidneys, you can also prepare small lamb rib chops in this way.

SERVES *4–6*

2¼ lb lamb kidneys
1¼ cups olive oil
⅔ cup white wine vinegar
a handful of fresh rosemary sprigs
salt and freshly ground pepper

Trim and rinse the kidneys carefully and cut them into neat slices. Mix the oil, vinegar, and rosemary together in a shallow dish and lay the kidney slices in the mixture. Leave to marinate at least 1 hour.

Remove the kidneys from the marinade and grill or broil about 5–7 minutes on each side, brushing them with a branch of rosemary dipped in the remaining marinade as they cook. Sprinkle the kidneys with salt and pepper just before serving.

FARMHOUSE STORE *Baskets of freshly harvested citrus fruits are loaded into a cart, ready to be taken to market.*

ALBANESI

Albanian Cookies

MAKES 20

1 wineglass of white wine
1 wineglass of olive oil
1 wineglass of sugar
all-purpose flour – as required
sugar for dusting
oil for greasing

Put the wine in a saucepan and add the oil. Bring to a boil, then add the sugar and stir until the sugar has dissolved. Stir in as much flour as the liquid will absorb, to make a smooth ball of dough rather like choux pastry. Tip it onto the work top and let it cool down.

Divide the dough into about 20 pieces and roll each one into a pencil shape with your hands, then roll it around into a ring shape. Dip the rings in sugar and arrange on an oiled baking sheet. Bake in a preheated moderately hot oven (400°F) about 12–15 minutes or until golden brown. Cool on a wire rack. Serve the cookies with sparkling wine.

LA FESTA DI SAN GIUSEPPE

Giuseppe's Name Day

When virtually everyone in Italy was named after a saint, your Name Day fell on the saint's day and the celebration would be almost the same as your birthday. Nowadays, Italian children are baptized with a much wider variety of names of very different origins, so there are fewer Name Day celebrations than there used to be.

San Giuseppe, or Saint Joseph, is one of Italy's most popular saints. I had looked forward very much to celebrating my friend Giuseppe's Name Day with him and his family on March 19. He was one of the first people to teach me about cooking and has always, as long as I can remember, refused to eat pre-packaged food, long before any theory that preservatives and colorings were perhaps not so wonderful after all. The olives with which we began his celebratory lunch, for instance, had been picked and bottled by Giuseppe himself to his own

recipe. Because he grows most of his own herbs and vegetables, everything he makes tastes incredibly fresh and delicious.

His minestrone is legendary and he always waxes lyrical about how healthy it is because it's fat-free. Having been raised on it from the age of three months, I can certainly vouch for that.

He insisted on making his *fegato alla Veneziana*, although his wife

complained that she would have liked to do it for him. He let her make the mashed potatoes instead! I had the job of picking the tiny, first-of-the-season salad leaves which we ate with a perfect balsamic vinegar dressing. To finish off, Giulia, Giuseppe's mother-in-law, made him a wonderfully golden, eggy rice cake. There was only one thing left to do at this point, which was to aid the digestion of this wonderful meal with some of Giuseppe's own home-distilled grappa . . .

Menu

Olive Nere Marinate

Il Grande Minestrone Vegetale

Il Fegato alla Veneziana or *La Pizzaiola*

Insalatina all'Aceto Balsamico

Purè di Patate al Limone

Crostata di Marmellata or *La Torta di Riso di Giulia*

EARLY SPRING IN THE VENETO (left) *Weak rays of sunshine brighten a March day.*

NAME DAY CAKES (left) *You may well receive a special cake on your Name Day – rather like a birthday.*

OLIVE NERE MARINATE

Marinated Black Olives

2¼ lb black olives
2 cups best quality olive oil
6 cloves garlic, crushed, then coarsely chopped
1 small red chili pepper, finely chopped
a handful of fresh rosemary sprigs, leaves removed
and chopped
salt and freshly ground pepper

If the olives are fresh (i.e. picked off the tree) they must be soaked in cold water 40 days, changing the water twice a day, in order to remove all the bitterness. If you are not using fresh olives, try to get olives preserved in brine; soak them in cold water overnight to remove the flavor of the brine. In both cases, rinse and dry the olives well once they have been appropriately soaked.

When the olives are ready, pack them into one or more large glass jars with tight-fitting lids. Mix the oil with all the other ingredients and pour it over the olives. The olives should be coated with oil but not swimming in it. Close the jars tightly and shake them to distribute the oil as evenly as possible. Keep in a cool place and use as required.

The olives improve with time but must be eaten within 3 months once opened. Serve as a delicious appetizer with wine and chunks of coarse bread to soak up the oil.

IL GRANDE MINESTRONE VEGETALE

Grand Vegetable Minestrone

SERVES 6

3 large carrots, diced
5–6 potatoes, peeled and diced
a handful of fresh spinach, chard or cabbage leaves,
washed and shredded finely
2 large stalks celery, sliced
1 large onion, chopped
1 large clove garlic, chopped
a handful of fresh parsley, washed and chopped
about 1 quart water
salt and freshly ground pepper
2 vegetable bouillon cubes or 2 teaspoons vegetable
extract
3 tablespoons tomato paste or 5 tablespoons chopped
canned tomatoes
olive oil to taste
about 8 leaves of fresh basil, torn into pieces

Make sure all the vegetables are shredded finely or chopped neatly into very small cubes and place them, with the garlic and parsley, in a large pot. Add about 1 quart of cold water plus a pinch of salt, pepper, the bouillon cubes or vegetable extract and the tomato paste or chopped canned tomatoes. Cover and simmer gently 1–2 hours, stirring occasionally.

When all the vegetables are soft and tender, remove from the heat. Just before serving, add olive oil and basil to taste – simply stir them into the soup without further cooking.

This soup can be served warm or cold but *never* hot. Parmesan cheese is superfluous.

Slice the onions very finely and rinse them thoroughly in cold water, before frying them with the sage leaves.

IL FEGATO ALLA VENEZIANA

Venetian Liver and Onions

SERVES 6–8

5 medium-sized onions, very finely sliced
3 walnut-sized pieces of butter
3 fresh sage leaves, rubbed
salt and freshly ground pepper
1 tablespoon vegetable oil
12 very thin, neat slices of calves' liver
purè di patate al limone *(see p.36)*

Rinse the onions thoroughly in cold water, then dry them with paper towel. Melt about 2 pieces of the butter in a wide pan with the sage and fry the onions until soft. Add salt and pepper to taste. Remove from the heat and set aside, but keep warm.

Melt the remaining butter in another wide pan with the oil and fry the liver very quickly, about 2–3 minutes each side. Season with salt and pepper and remove from the heat.

To serve, arrange the mashed potato on a platter, put the onions on top and the liver on top of them. Serve at once.

Fry the slices of liver very quickly. 2–3 minutes on each side is enough.

35

LA PIZZAIOLA

Beef Pizzaiola

SERVES 6

6 very thin boneless sirloin steaks, trimmed of all fat
and gristle
4 cloves garlic, finely chopped
4 tablespoons olive oil
16 oz canned crushed tomatoes or tomato purée
or a mixture of the two
½ heaped teaspoon dried oregano
½ heaped teaspoon pesto sauce or 1 tablespoon
chopped fresh basil
salt and freshly ground pepper

You may need to use 2 skillets or to make this dish in 2 batches.

Pound the steaks until very thin with a meat pounder. Heat the garlic and olive oil together in a wide pan over a medium heat until the garlic is golden brown. Add the tomatoes and bring to a boil. Cook about 5 minutes, stirring frequently.

Stir in the oregano and pesto or basil, then slide in the beef. Cook a maximum of 2 minutes on each side, then remove from the heat. Season to taste with salt and pepper and transfer to a dish to serve.

This dish is excellent with mashed or boiled potatoes and a green salad.

FRESH FROM THE GARDEN (right) *Tiny young salad leaves from the first crop of the season are what make this simple salad special.*

INSALATINA ALL' ACETO BALSAMICO

Tiny Salad Leaves with Balsamic Vinegar Dressing

SERVES 6–8

4–5 handfuls of very young salad leaves including
lettuce, arugula, Belgian endive, etc.
1½ teaspoons balsamic vinegar
½ teaspoon salt
¼ teaspoon white pepper
6 tablespoons olive oil

Wash and dry the salad leaves very carefully and arrange in a bowl.

Mix the balsamic vinegar with the salt until the salt has dissolved, then stir in the pepper and olive oil.

Taste the dressing to check it is correctly seasoned for your taste, then pour onto the salad. Toss everything together and serve.

PURÈ DI PATATE AL LIMONE

Mashed Potato with Lemon

SERVES 6–8

6 large potatoes suitable for mashing
1¼ cups milk
1¼ cups water
salt and freshly ground pepper
2-4 tablespoons unsalted butter
grated rind of 1 very large lemon or 2 smaller ones

Peel the potatoes and cut them into equal-sized pieces. Put them into a saucepan and cover with the milk and the water. Add a large pinch of salt. Bring to a boil and simmer them gently until soft.

Drain off all excess liquid and mash carefully with a fork, then push through a potato ricer to make a really smooth purée. Stir in the butter, the lemon rind and pepper to taste. Serve at once, or reheat the purée briefly just before serving.

TILED KITCHEN (right) *Still lifes and kitchen implements combine the aesthetic and the practical in a typically Italian way.*

CROSTATA DI MARMELLATA

Plum Jam and Amaretto Tart

MAKES ONE *12-INCH TART*

Pastry
3½ cups all-purpose plain flour
¾ cup sugar
11 oz (2¾ sticks) butter
3 egg yolks
a pinch of salt
butter for greasing

Filling
a 1–lb jar sour plum or sour cherry jam
6-8 amaretti cookies, broken up
1 heaped tablespoon unsweetened cocoa
confectioners' sugar for dusting

Sift the flour onto the work top in a pile and make a hole in the center; put the sugar and butter into this hole with the egg yolks and salt. Blend everything together quickly with your fingertips (do not knead). When it is an amalgamated ball, put it in a plastic bag and let rest in the refrigerator about 30 minutes.

Mix the jam, amaretti cookies and cocoa together until smooth. Roll out the pastry fairly thick. Use to line a buttered 12-inch loose-bottomed tart pan. Press down around the edges to create a crust. Spoon the jam filling into the center and smooth it out. Roll out the pastry trimmings and cut into rounds. Arrange on top of the filling.

Bake in a preheated moderately hot oven (400°F) 20 minutes, then turn down to 350°F and bake a further 20-25 minutes, or until golden brown. Remove from the oven and cool. Dust the top with confectioners' sugar before serving.

LA TORTA DI RISO DI GIULIA

Giulia's Rice Cake

MAKES ONE 10-INCH CAKE

¾ *cup short-grain rice*
4¾ *cups milk*
butter for greasing
2 tablespoons semolina
8 eggs
2 cups sugar
3 tablespoons brandy
juice of ½ lemon or grated rind of ½ lemon

Put the rice and 2¾ cups of the milk in a saucepan and bring to a boil. Cook 10 minutes, then drain.

Butter a deep 10-inch cake pan thoroughly and scatter the semolina over the butter. Do not use a loose-bottomed pan or the liquid will ooze out. Turn the cake pan upside-down to remove any loose semolina.

Beat the eggs in a large bowl until foaming and pale yellow. Add the sugar a little at a time, beating constantly, followed by the brandy and the lemon juice or rind. Stir very thoroughly before adding the rice and the remaining 2 cups of milk. Pour the mixture into the cake pan.

Bake in the center of a preheated moderate oven (350°F) about 50 minutes or until a wooden toothpick inserted into the center comes out clean. The cake should be set and golden brown. Serve warm or cold.

KITCHEN UTENSILS (left)

LA TORTA DI RISO DI GIULIA (right)

Butter the cake pan thoroughly before scattering in the semolina.

Stir the egg mixture well before adding the rice and remaining milk.

UN PICNIC LUNIGIANO

Tuscan Picnic

Although I was born and educated in Rome, my summers were spent in Tuscany where my parents and other branches of the family had villas. The family estates encompassed sprawling vineyards and silver-gray olive groves, which in my mother's time yielded olives that at harvest time were pressed to make the estate's own oil. It is from this landscape of rolling, umber-colored hills, endless vineyards, and intense blue seas that my happiest and most vivid memories come. In returning to Tuscany I slip back instantly into this land and its way of life with the very deepest sense of having come home.

One day in May, I decided to take my own children back to one of the picnic haunts of my childhood. Picnicking is something Italians do a lot. Weather permitting, on *Pasquetta*, Easter Monday, the entire family including grandmama, newborn baby and all, set off for the countryside for the annual *scampagnata*, or outing. And during the summer months many families take to the cool of the shady hills and hold their picnics there, often lighting dan-

gerous fires on which they cook their pasta. These cooking fires can be a problem if not built safely and the buzz of summer insects is often drowned by the buzz of mountain patrol helicopters during these months.

When I was a child, my parents used to organize picnics for me and my brothers as often as possible during the warm days. We would always choose a site that was near cool running water and in a place where we were allowed to light a safe fire, so that we could enjoy one of the real picnic treats – freshly cooked pasta – in the open air.

On the day I took my own children off for a picnic, the spot I chose was down by the river and to get there we had to park the cars some way off and then wind our way through the long grass and poppies all the way to the river bank. We found a narrow

THE PASTA POT *Spaghetti cooked out of doors on an open fire and served with even the simplest sauce or dressing always tastes surprisingly good.*

strip of land covered in cool, soft green grass that jutted out into the river and a nearby wooden jetty which was perfect for laying out the food. As we had quite a lot to carry, the walk was arduous enough to make getting there worthwhile, and cool dips in the river were definitely the first item on the agenda.

The next task was to select some flat white stones to make a secure circle for the fire. We then built our fire in the center, using all the odd bits of driftwood we could find. Once we had glowing red embers, the grill was laid on top and the water could then be boiled for our pasta.

Eating pasta which has been cooked out of doors under a summer sky is one of the most delicious experiences. All you need is a pot, enough fresh, clean water in which to cook the spaghetti, and some salt. I chose a very simple oil and garlic dressing for this picnic, but you can take along a ready-made sauce of any kind you prefer.

As well as the menu listed here, I also took plenty of bread and Parma ham, salami, Parmesan cheese in chunks, firm red toma-toes, and fresh fruit. Many Italian foods seem almost made for picnics with the wealth of different cold meats and cheeses, breads like focaccia, which can be split open to make envelopes into

YOUNG ROMANS *Voluminous towels and a bush of wild sage growing nearby provided the props for this impromptu re-enactment of the Roman Empire.*

which any number of fillings can be stuffed, and the quality of fresh vegetables and fruit which need no further preparation. Having said that, preparing some simple dishes at home or packing the ingredients to combine at the picnic spot adds a far more special touch to the occasion, and all the food I prepared and took along for this picnic was ideal for hearty, outdoor appetites. Fresh fruit provided a suitably refreshing conclusion to the meal – pear slices dipped into creamy mascarpone cheese and luxurious soft peaches soaked in lots of red wine.

After lunch, my sons dressed up as Roman Emperors with crowns of wild sage around their heads and then we waded downstream on an exploration trip. On the river bank the boys soon discovered a hunter's shelter made out of green boughs and we nestled inside, with me telling them stories of the picnics of my own childhood – until they got hungry again and we had to go and eat up the rest of the picnic.

Menu

Spaghetti Aglio e Olio

Mozzarella con Verdura Mista

Frittata di Cipolla

Insalata di Pollo

Pane, Fichi e Alici

Pesche al Vino

Mascarpone con le Pere

SPAGHETTI AGLIO E OLIO

Spaghetti with Oil and Garlic

SERVES *6*

1 lb fine spaghetti or spaghettini
salt and freshly ground pepper
2–5 cloves garlic, minced
about 1 cup olive oil
1 dried small red chili pepper (optional)

First light the fire. Let the flames die down and then make sure you have a good constant base of hot embers and low flames which are required for boiling water. If the fire is surrounded by stones, you can lay the grill over the fire so that it rests flat on the stones; put the pot of salted water on the top. Put a lid on the pot and bring the water to a boil. Toss in the spaghetti, stir to prevent sticking, and cook until *al dente.*

Meanwhile, put the garlic and oil into a small pan and heat them together over the fire, next to the boiling pot of spaghetti. The garlic should go really dark brown and crispy. If you want to, you can put the chili pepper in with the garlic as well.

When the garlic is blackened, throw it away (the same applies to the chili). By now, the spaghetti must be ready to drain. Holding the lid on firmly, tip the pot over and pour out the water, but not the spaghetti (alternatively, pack a colander). Try to drain the pasta fairly well. Pour the flavored oil into the pot and toss with the spaghetti using 2 forks. (If you have not used the chili, season with freshly ground black pepper.) Serve at once.

MOZZARELLA CON VERDURA MISTA

Mozzarella with Mixed Vegetables

SERVES *6*

12 slices of Marmande or other large flavorful tomato
12 slices of mozzarella cheese (same size as the tomato)
1½ cups chopped vegetables to include scallions, sweet peppers, zucchini, carrots, and cucumbers
⅓ cup capers, rinsed and dried carefully
about ½ cup olive oil
salt and freshly ground pepper

Arrange the tomato slices on a wide platter or in boxes and cover with the mozzarella slices. Cover each one with a little of the chopped mixed vegetables. Arrange the capers on top, then douse each one with olive oil and sprinkle with salt and pepper. Cover tightly to take on the picnic. Alternatively, take all the ingredients prepared in advance and put them all together at the last minute.

FRITTATA DI CIPOLLA

Flat Onion Omelette

This is one to make at home and take with you to eat cold.

SERVES *6*

10 eggs, beaten
salt and freshly ground pepper
3 large onions, thinly sliced
½ cup olive oil

Beat the eggs very thoroughly with plenty of salt and pepper. Rinse and dry the sliced onions thoroughly. Heat half the olive oil in a large skillet and fry the onions until soft, stirring occasionally, without allowing them to brown. Cool the cooked onions and season with a little salt. Tip the cooked, cold onions into the egg mixture.

Wipe the skillet completely clean and pour the remaining oil into it. Heat the oil until smoking hot, then tip the egg and onion mixture into the pan. Fry on one side 3–5 minutes or until browned and fairly firm. Place a large lid or plate on the pan and turn the omelette out onto the lid or plate, so that it comes out upside-down. Slide it back into the pan the other way up so that the uncooked side can brown and firm. Unmold it again in the same way, cool, and serve cut in wedges.

MOZZARELLA CON VERDURA MISTA (left),
FRITTATA DI CIPOLLA (right)

INSALATA DI POLLO

Chicken Salad

To prevent the salad leaves from becoming soggy, take the washed and dried endive with you in one container and the marinating chicken in another. You can then put the two together at the last minute on a wide plastic tray.

SERVES 6

⅓ cup golden raisins
3–4 skinned chicken breast halves, boiled
2 teaspoons grated lemon rind
5 tablespoons oil
juice of 2 lemons
3 tablespoons chopped fresh parsley
salt
1 head curly endive

Soak the raisins in cold water about 20 minutes. Slice the chicken breasts thinly and put them in a bowl. Mix the oil and lemon juice together, then add the parsley, lemon rind, and salt to taste. Cover the chicken breasts with this marinade.

Drain the raisins, scatter them over the chicken, and mix everything together. Cover and marinate until required, then serve on a bed of curly endive.

PANE, FICHI E ALICI

Bread, Figs, and Anchovies

*Take the whole loaf of bread and cut it at the picnic,
but prepare the rest of the ingredients beforehand and
take them packed in boxes.*

SERVES 6

6–8 fillets of salted or canned anchovies, rinsed
thoroughly
1¼ lb fresh, ripe figs, peeled
2 cloves garlic, very finely chopped
6 thick slices of bread
about 6 tablespoons olive oil
4 scallions, finely chopped

Make sure all of the salt has been washed off
the anchovies, then remove any remaining
bones. If using canned anchovies, rinse them
thoroughly to remove all the oil. Mash the
anchovies and figs together (alternatively,
whizz in the food processor). Add the garlic.

Sprinkle the slices of bread with oil, spread
with the fig mixture, and scatter the scallions
on top. Any remaining oil can be drizzled over
the onion.

PESCE AL VINO (above), MASCARPONE CON LE
PERE (below)

PESCHE AL VINO

Peaches in Red Wine

*You can either let everybody do their own or prepare
a bowl of peaches in advance.
Other fruit such as pears and apricots are also good
served this way.*

SERVES 6

6–12 peaches (depending on how large they are)
about 2 cups dry red or white wine
sugar to taste (optional)

Slice the unpeeled peaches into the red wine.
Sprinkle with a little sugar if desired and leave
to macerate for as long as you like.

Eat the peaches first, then drink the wonderfully flavored wine – then fall asleep in the
shade!

MASCARPONE CON
LE PERE

Mascarpone with Pears

SERVES 6

6 ripe, firm pears
about ¾ lb (1½ cups) mascarpone cheese

Peel the pears and slice into easily holdable
pieces. Dip and scoop into the mascarpone as
your fancy takes you, or spread each piece of
pear thickly with the cheese and arrange them
all on a platter.

45

A PRANZO DA ELEONORA

Dinner with Eleonora

Sicily's best known and most respected cookery expert is my dear friend Eleonora Consoli. I first met Eleonora through the Count and Countess Notabartolo on their estate at Lentini, when we spent time there filming for my cookery series for BBC television, and we have been friends ever since. I simply cannot visit the island without seeing her and my last visit was no exception.

As usual, Eleonora was organizing some kind of get-together and invited me along. It turned out to be a girls' night, in honor of the *Festa della Donna*, the day when all of Italy celebrates women. It seemed slightly out of place to be celebrating this in Sicily, where many advances which women elsewhere take for granted still present an uphill struggle, but I was happy just to be in Eleonora's company again.

APERITIFS BEFORE DINNER (right)
Dinner with Eleonora Consoli, who presents her own cookery program on Italy's RAI channel, guarantees not only delicious, but also extremely interesting food.

It is a wonderful thing to discover in another cook the same passion and drive about food that I feel. Eleonora has taught me so much about the food of Sicily and its myriad traditions, and her love for her island and its cuisine is absolutely infectious. Because she knows how I want to enlarge my repertoire of Sicilian cooking, on this evening she prepared dishes with which I was not familiar. We began with the *timballo del Gattopardo*, the Leopard's timbale – an allusion to the prince of that name in Lampedusa's novel *The Leopard*, which evokes the enchanting lost world of the Sicilian nobility of the last century. It is a typical baroque dish, so characteristic of Sicily in being gloriously complicated and rich.

Menu

Il Timballo del Gattopardo

Nasello al Gratin

Nidi di Scuma

Falsomagro al Sugo

Gelo di Cannella

Eleonora then prepared a delicious scrod. Because nothing in Sicilian cuisine is ever really simple – though it may deceive you into thinking that it is – surrounding the fish were deep-fried nests of pasta filled with fresh peas. The quintessential Sicilian meat dish followed – *il falsomagro*, literally "fake lean."

When Eleonora brought out the dessert she smiled at me – she knows just how much I adore this delightfully refreshing cinnamon-flavored mold. As she sat down at the table she whispered quietly to me, "It was the Leopard's favorite dessert, too!"

IL TIMBALLO DEL GATTOPARDO
Enjoyed against the superb backdrop of Palermo, the dinner evoked the magical world of Lampedusa's Sicily.

IL TIMBALLO DEL GATTOPARDO

The Leopard's Timbale

SERVES 8

Pastry

3½ cups all-purpose flour
9 oz (2¼ sticks) unsalted butter
10 tablespoons sugar
3 eggs
a pinch of salt
1 teaspoon grated lemon rind

Filling

9 tablespoons olive oil
2 onions, chopped
1½ cups shelled fresh peas or frozen petite peas
½ lb boneless sirloin steak, trimmed and chopped coarsely
1½ cups beef stock
½ lb chicken livers
1 clove
salt and freshly ground pepper
¾ lb elbow macaroni
2 hard-cooked eggs, shelled and chopped
5–6 tablespoons ricotta or other fresh soft cheese
¾ lb cooked ham, chopped
½ cup freshly grated Parmesan cheese
2 egg yolks, beaten

To make the pastry, sift the flour onto the work top in a pile and plunge your fist into the center to make a hole; put the butter and sugar into this hole with the eggs, salt, and grated lemon rind. Blend all these ingredients together quickly with your fingertips to make a smooth ball of dough. Be careful not to knead it too much or it will become heavy. Put the dough in a bowl, cover with a cloth, and chill until required.

For the filling, heat half the olive oil in a saucepan and fry one of the onions with the peas until soft. Add the meat. Cover and simmer gently about 20 minutes, adding the stock gradually.

Meanwhile, fry the other onion in the remaining olive oil in a skillet about 5 minutes. Add the chicken livers and the clove and cook everything briefly until the chicken livers have become slightly crumbly. Season with salt and pepper to taste. Remove from the heat and set aside.

Bring a large pot of salted water to a boil and cook the macaroni until *al dente* (check package for cooking time as brands vary). Drain the pasta and dress it with the juices from the meat and pea sauce.

Roll out two-thirds of the dough to a thickness of about ¼ inch and use to line a greased deep 10-inch cake pan. Put a layer of macaroni on the bottom, then cover with alternating layers of peas and steak, chicken livers, hard-cooked egg, ricotta, and chopped ham. Continue to layer until you fill the pastry case, sprinkling the layers from time to time with grated Parmesan.

Roll out the remaining dough and cut out a round to fit the top of the pan. Lay the dough over the filling, and pinch the edges together securely to seal. Brush with the beaten egg yolks and pierce the top in several places to let the steam escape.

Bake in a preheated moderately hot oven (375°F) for about 1 hour or until the pastry is golden brown.

Let the timbale stand in its pan about 10–15 minutes after it comes out of the oven: the pie crust will then pull away from the side of the pan, making it easier to serve. Serve directly from the pan or unmold the timbale carefully onto a platter.

NASELLO AL GRATIN

Baked Scrod

SERVES 6

1 whole scrod (baby cod) or other white fish such as whiting, weighing about 2 ¼ lb, drawn
2½ cups fresh bread crumbs
½ cup chopped fresh parsley
salt and freshly ground pepper
5 tablespoons olive oil
2–oz can anchovies, drained
juice of 2 lemons

Open the fish out flat as much as possible, placing it on its back in a baking dish. Cover the fish with about half the bread crumbs, half the parsley, and salt and pepper to taste. Heat the oil in a small pan and add the anchovies, mashing them in the hot oil to make a smooth sauce. (Alternatively, blend the anchovies and oil in a food processor.) Pour this all over the fish and cover with the remaining bread crumbs and parsley.

Bake in a preheated moderate oven (350°F) 30–40 minutes or until the fish will flake easily when tested with a fork. Sprinkle over the lemon juice and serve.

NIDI DI SCUMA

Fried Pasta Nests

SERVES 4–6

*½ lb fine capellini pasta nests
salt
oil for deep frying
about 2 cups cooked vegetables, such as peas,
onions, or mushrooms*

Bring a large pot of salted water to a boil. Toss in the pasta nests and cook until *al dente* (check package for cooking time as brands vary). Drain and allow to cook until just lukewarm.

Heat a large pan of oil until a small piece of bread dropped into it sizzles instantly. Reshape the cooked noodles into nest shapes, by twisting them around a fork. Using a slotted spoon, lower them into the hot oil, one or two at a time. Let them fry until crisp and golden, then remove with a slotted spoon and drain on paper towels to remove excess oil.

Fill these nests with freshly cooked vegetables of your choice, such as braised peas and onions, braised mushrooms or artichokes, stewed zucchini or sweet peppers. Serve hot.

FILLING THE PASTA NESTS *Any cooked vegetables – on this occasion we had braised peas – can be used to fill the pasta nests.*

FALSOMAGRO AL SUGO

Sicilian Stuffed Meat Roll

SERVES 6

1½ lb boneless veal in one large, thick slice
¾ lb ground veal
1¾ cups fresh bread crumbs
¾ cup freshly grated caciocavallo
or Parmesan cheese,
2 hard-cooked eggs, shelled and chopped
1 egg
salt and freshly ground pepper
freshly grated nutmeg or ground cinnamon
2 oz tuna, provola, or provolone cheese, sliced
2 oz mortadella or salame
4–6 tablespoons olive oil
1 onion, chopped
1 carrot, chopped
1 stalk celery, chopped
2 heaped tablespoons tomato paste
16-oz can tomatoes
1 clove
⅔ cup dry red wine

Using a meat pounder, flatten the slice of veal as much as possible to make one large, very thin sheet of meat. If necessary, use more than one slice and overlap them as you use the pounder to create a similar effect. Place the sheet of meat on a wet cloth or dish towel.

Mix the ground veal thoroughly with the bread crumbs and caciocavallo or Parmesan. Add to this mixture the two chopped hard-cooked eggs and the raw egg to bind the stuffing together. Season with salt, pepper, and nutmeg or cinnamon.

Before the ingredients are piled up on top, it is important that the veal used for falsomagro *has been flattened until it is as thin as possible; otherwise the roll will be too thick.*

FALSOMAGRO, *served with a tomato sauce. This stuffed meat roll, which is equally delicious served hot or cold, is a typically Sicilian dish in its richness and elaborateness.*

Spread the stuffing over the meat, leaving a border around the edges. Cover the stuffing with the slices of tuma, provola, or provolone and then with the slices of mortadella or salame. Roll the meat up lengthwise like a jelly roll, using the wet cloth or dish towel to help and drawing the ends together very tightly in order to squeeze the roll closed. Remove the cloth carefully and tie the roll securely with kitchen string.

Heat the olive oil in a wide saucepan and fry the chopped onion, carrot, and celery until the onion is soft and translucent. Moisten with a little water every now and again. (Instead of water you could use the juice from the canned tomatoes.) Stir in the tomato paste. Cook about 10 minutes, then add the drained, chopped tomatoes and clove. Season with salt, pepper, and nutmeg or cinnamon and continue to simmer gently about 15 minutes.

Lay the meat roll in the pan and spoon the sauce all over it – as though you were basting the meat. Pour in the red wine and allow the fumes to evaporate, then add enough water just to cover the meat. Cover the pan and simmer very gently about 1½ hours. Check the pan occasionally and if necessary add more water to the meat as it simmers.

To serve, remove the meat roll from the pan and take off the string. Slice the meat thinly and arrange it on a platter. Reduce the sauce in the pan over a lively heat, until it has reduced by about half, then pour it all over the sliced meat. Serve hot or cold.

GELO DI CANNELLA

Cinnamon Mold

SERVES 6

⅓ oz cinnamon sticks
3¼ cups cold water
1½ cups sugar
½ cup cornstarch
2 squares semisweet chocolate, finely chopped
(optional)

Put the cinnamon sticks and cold water into a saucepan. Place over a medium heat and bring to a boil, then boil gently about 5 minutes. Remove from the heat and let stand 12 hours.

Strain the cinnamon liquid carefully and return to the pan. Add the sugar. Dissolve the cornstarch in 2 tablespoons of the cinnamon liquid and add to the rest of the ingredients in the pan. Bring to a boil, stirring constantly, and boil very gently until thickened. Remove from the heat and add the chocolate if using. Stir until the chocolate has melted.

Turn into one large or 6 small individual molds and chill until solid. Unmold to serve, decorated with lemon leaves.

GELO DI CANNELLA (left) *decorated with strawberries, cherries, and apricots.*

IN THE KITCHEN (far left) *Eleonora (in the foreground) had us all involved in the preparations.*

LA BISTECCATA

A Barbecue in Ronchi

If you are lucky enough to have your barbecue in a beautiful setting, and have access to plenty of scented, pungent wood which will lend wonderful flavors to your food, then I think you are on the way to having the most delicious of all meals. Food always tastes better out of doors in any case, and the effort of lighting the fire, cutting the wood into a suitable size, and tending the fire and the food throughout the whole operation does wonders for the appetite.

All over Italy tremendous importance is placed on the wood used to make the fire. In Sicily, for example, they like to use lemon wood because it gives the food a unique citrus flavor. In Alto Adige, larch is used to cook polenta because it gives the finished dish such a deliciously smoky taste. At home in Tuscany we always use pine cones to get the fire going, and then use a combination of pine and apple wood for the actual cooking. I often throw some herbs on the fire, too, to add a special flavor to the food – fresh rosemary is wonderful with lamb and dried bay leaves really add to beef.

The disadvantage – and advantage – with our barbecue is that it is a permanent construction of stone, wood, and cement with an extremely deep hole in the top where the fire is built. This means that the fire really does have to be enormous, so it's never worth having a barbecue unless we are cooking huge amounts of food! If we are having a barbecue at lunchtime, for example, we need to get the fire lit by about 10 o'clock in the morning.

If it is at all possible, even if you are only using charcoal, having more than one fire going, with separate grills – or a very wide fire with more than one grill, so that you can cook lots of different things without the flavors becoming mixed up. In this menu, you could put all the meat onto one grill and cook the mussel kebabs on a different grill over the same fire. (You could also cook the kebabs on one of those grills specially made for cooking small fish, which save them from dropping straight into the burning embers. This is not essential, but it will make life a lot easier.) When I cook a barbecue with so many different flavors, I ask someone to bring their portable barbecue along to ease matters.

The best thing about a barbecue is that there will always be plenty of joining. The more people who become involved, the more fun the event will be – and the less work there will be for the cook. It is quite strange how even the most kitchen-shy man will become a fully qualified chef once he's within feet of the barbecue. Maybe it's something to do with age-old instincts and mammoth hunting, but I think that if a man (or a group of men) wants to take care of the cooking at a barbecue, then he should be encouraged to do so!

The best piece of advice I was ever given regarding the success of a barbecue is this – make sure the table at which everyone is eating is a good long way from the fire. Although you'll have further to walk back and forth with the food, you won't risk smoking anybody out and you give the cook – or cooks – plenty of space.

Menu

Spiedini di Cozze

Hamburger all'Italiana

Hamburger Piccanti

Abbacchio a Scottadito

Spiedini d'Agnello con Peperone

Spiedini di Manzo

Radicchio ai Ferri

Peperoni ai Ferri

Bruschetta

Banane al Cioccolato

GRILLING HAMBURGERS (left) *If you are fortunate enough to have such a large barbecue you can cook food with very different flavors.*

SPIEDINI D'AGNELLO CON PEPERONE (left)

SPIEDINI DI COZZE

Mussel Kebabs

SERVES 6

6 dozen mussels
½ lb bacon, sliced as thinly as possible
4 cloves garlic, finely chopped
5 tablespoons very finely chopped fresh parsley
salt and freshly ground pepper
2 eggs, beaten
¾–1 cup fresh bread crumbs

Scrub and clean the mussels thoroughly, being sure to remove the beard. Place them all in a wide pan and put over a lively heat with the lid on. Give them about 5 minutes to open up, shaking the pan occasionally to help them open, then remove from the heat. Discard any mussels that have not opened and remove the others from their shells.

Cut the slices of bacon into squares of about the same size as the mussels. Arrange the mussels and bacon squares alternately on kebab skewers.

Mix the garlic and parsley together with the bread crumbs and add a little salt and pepper. Roll the kebabs in the beaten egg then in the bread crumb mixture. Grill them on the barbecue over a gentle heat about 3 minutes on each side or until crisp. Serve hot.

STEAMED MUSSELS *A barbecue does not have to consist of all meat.*

HAMBURGER ALL'ITALIANA

Italian Hamburgers

SERVES 6

2¼ lb lean ground beef
1 cup pitted green olives, sliced or chopped
1 onion, chopped
1 egg
salt and freshly ground pepper
3 tablespoons olive oil

Mix together the beef, olives, onion, egg, and salt and pepper to taste. Shape into 6 flat, thick disks. Brush with olive oil on both sides.

Grill on the barbecue over a medium heat about 4 minutes on each side.

HAMBURGER PICCANTI

Hamburgers with Chili

SERVES 6

2¼ lb lean ground beef
3 eggs
a large pinch of chili powder (or more to taste)
2 tablespoons capers, rinsed and chopped
a pinch of dried mint
2–3 tablespoons freshly grated Parmesan cheese
salt
3 tablespoons olive oil

Mix the ground beef with the eggs, chili powder, capers, mint, cheese, and salt to taste. Shape into 6 flat, thick disks and brush them on both sides with oil.

Grill on the barbecue over a medium heat about 4 minutes on each side.

Serve with a crisp salad or with lots of fresh crusty bread.

SPIEDINI DI COZZE (left)

FRESH ROSEMARY (right) *Throw some fresh rosemary onto the fire as the lamb cooks; it will give it a very special flavor.*

ABBACHIO A SCOTTADITO

"Burn your Fingers" Lamb Chops

SERVES 6

12 small lamb rib chops
2 cloves garlic
salt and freshly ground pepper
4 tablespoons olive oil

Rub the chops all over with the peeled garlic and sprinkle generously with salt and freshly ground pepper.

Grill on the barbecue over a medium heat 3–4 minutes on each side, brushing liberally with olive oil as they cook.

SPIEDINI D'AGNELLO CON PEPERONE

Lamb Kebabs with Green Peppers

SERVES 6–8

2¼ lb boned shoulder of lamb
2 green sweet peppers

*salt and freshly ground pepper
branches of fresh rosemary
1 wineglass of olive oil*

Cut the meat into quite wide and thick chunks – about 1¾ inch wide and at least 1¼ inch thick. Cut the peppers in half, remove the seeds and the membranes, and cut into equal-sized pieces. Thread the meat and the peppers alternately onto kebab sticks or sticks of scented wood such as rosemary or bay which you can whittle especially for this dish. Make sure you pack everything very tightly onto the sticks. Season generously with salt and pepper.

Grill on the barbecue over a medium heat about 6 minutes on each side. While the kebabs cook, dip the branches of rosemary into the olive oil and brush over the meat frequently. Serve very hot.

SPIEDINI D'AGNELLO CON PEPERONE

SPIEDINI DI MANZO

Beef Kebabs

Throw some dried bay leaves onto the fire to impart a special flavor to the meat.

SERVES 6

1 yellow sweet pepper
2¼ lb lean beef steak, cut into equal-sized chunks
2 onions, cut into quarters
about 18 mushrooms preserved in olive oil, or
button mushrooms
about 20 black olives, pitted
about 12 bay leaves
salt and freshly ground pepper
4 tablespoons olive oil

Bring a pan of water to a boil, toss in the sweet pepper, and blanch about 3 minutes. Drain, then cut into strips, removing all the seeds and membrane.

Alternate the chunks of beef on kebab skewers with pieces of onion, mushrooms, slices of yellow pepper, olives, and bay leaves. Sprinkle with salt and pepper, then baste generously with oil.

Grill on the barbecue over a medium to high heat about 4 minutes on each side.

RADICCHIO AI FERRI (right) *Other vegetables such as eggplant and fennel can be coated with oil and grilled in this way, too.*

RADICCHIO AI FERRI

Grilled Radicchio

SERVES 6

3 large firm heads of radicchio, with as much root or
base as possible
9 tablespoons olive oil
salt
freshly ground pepper

Cut the heads of radicchio in half and wash all 6 pieces carefully. Shake them dry, holding them by the base. Mix the olive oil and salt and pepper together and immerse the radicchio in the oil; be sure they are well coated.

Grill the radicchio on the barbecue over a medium heat about 4 minutes on each side, pressing down firmly to flatten them as much as possible.

Make sure the metal of the grill is thoroughly hot before you begin to cook, otherwise the radicchio will fall apart.

PEPERONI AI FERRI

Grilled Sweet Peppers

SERVES 6

4 large, fleshy sweet peppers, any color
salt
6–8 tablespoons olive oil
3 cloves garlic, finely chopped
3 tablespoons chopped fresh parsley
freshly ground black pepper

Bring a large pot of salted water to a boil and toss in the whole peppers. Blanch about 2 minutes, then drain them. Cut them in half lengthwise, and remove all the seeds and membranes. Cut them in half again and brush all over with a little oil.

Grill them on the barbecue over medium heat about 2 minutes on each side or until just softened. Transfer them to a dish and sprinkle with the garlic, parsley, black pepper to taste, and remaining oil. Let marinate about 15 minutes before serving.

PEPERONI AI FERRI (left)

TENDING THE BARBECUE *The barbecue in my garden is so deep it takes hours to get the fire going, so it's only worth it if I cook huge amounts of food – the perfect excuse.*

BRUSCHETTA

Italian Barbecued Toast

SERVES 6

12 thick slices of pane ciabatta
2 cloves garlic
7 tablespoons olive oil
salt and freshly ground pepper

Toast the bread on both sides on the barbecue over a medium heat, then remove from the grill and rub generously all over with the peeled garlic. Drench with olive oil, sprinkle with salt and pepper, and serve quickly while it is still crisp and warm.

BANANE AL CIOCCOLATO

Chocolate Bananas

SERVES 6

6 large, firm bananas
6–7 squares semisweet or bittersweet chocolate,
chopped roughly

Slice open the bananas lengthwise without peeling them and without cutting them completely in half. Insert the chocolate along each slit. Close the peel around the bananas and wrap each one tightly in foil. Grill on the barbecue over a medium to low heat, turning them over halfway through cooking, about 6–8 minutes or until the bananas are soft and the chocolate runny. Serve with lots of soft Italian vanilla ice cream.

UNA COLAZIONE MILANESE

Chic Milanese Lunch

It doesn't seem to matter what I wear in Milan, I still feel utterly dowdy and completely under-dressed for any occasion. The lunch my cousin Gianluca gave at his apartment was no exception.

Being young and rich in Milan means having an elegant address, lots of equally elegant friends, and lots of money to spend on the good things in life. Milan has the best known *nouvelle cuisine* restaurant in Italy, owned and created by Gualtiero Marchesi. To my mind, this is the only Italian city in which such a restaurant could actually survive. The city has an extraordinary flair which I have never come across elsewhere in Italy, and only very rarely elsewhere in the world, and much of its considerable wealth seems to be happily spent on simply enjoying life.

Gianluca's lunch was typical of this philosophy. The food was beautifully presented and the company was beautifully but

GIANLUCA'S KITCHEN (right) *The antique, marble-topped dining table is the centerpiece of this elegant kitchen.*

unpretentiously dressed. In the elegant kitchen, with its antique central table, we began with a delicious combination of bright yellow Milanese risotto rice with asparagus. To follow, there were perfect deep-fried zucchini flowers and thin crêpes filled with a delightful mixture of spinach and ricotta. The crispy mozzarella *in carrozza*, literally "in a carriage," had been sandwiched in white bread and deep fried. Finally, there were fresh figs, beautifully arranged on top of a light zabaglione, to finish off the meal in a suitably stylish Milanese way.

Menu

Asparagi alla Milanese

Fiori di Zucchine

Crespelle di Ricotta e Spinaci

Mozzarella in Carrozza

Fichi Verdi con Zabaglione di Prosecco

LUNCH WITH FRIENDS (right) *Wealthy Milan puts a high priority on enjoying the good things in life.*

ASPARAGI ALLA MILANESE

Milanese Asparagus

SERVES 6

1 stick of butter
1 small onion, finely chopped
2½ cups risotto (arborio) rice
¾ cup dry white wine
salt and freshly ground pepper
2 quarts vegetable or chicken stock, kept hot
30 asparagus spears, trimmed
1 teaspoon saffron powder, or a large pinch of
saffron threads steeped in 4 tablespoons hot water
½ cup freshly grated Parmesan cheese
6 eggs

Melt half the butter in a heavy-bottomed saucepan and fry the onion until soft. Add the rice and stir to coat it with butter and onion. Add the wine and cook, stirring, until you can no longer smell the fumes from the alcohol.

Begin to add the stock, one ladleful at a time, stirring constantly to prevent sticking and to distribute the flavoring and the liquid equally. Never add more liquid until the previous quantity has been absorbed into the risotto. The risotto will take about 20 minutes to make from the moment that you add the rice to the onion.

FRESH ASPARAGUS (left) *Lombardy is noted for its excellent asparagus which grows in many areas around Milan.*

While the risotto is cooking, steam the asparagus until tender (about 11 minutes).

Five minutes before the risotto is finished, add the saffron powder or liquid and stir it in very thoroughly. Season to taste with salt and pepper. As soon as the rice is tender and properly swollen, add half the remaining butter and the Parmesan. Remove from the heat, cover, and let the risotto stand 2–3 minutes.

Meanwhile, heat the remaining butter in a big skillet and fry the 6 eggs until just set. (You may like to use more butter or oil.)

Arrange 5 asparagus spears on each of the six plates, spoon the yellow risotto in an attractive shape next to the asparagus, and cover with a fried egg. Serve at once.

FIORI DI ZUCCHINE

Deep-Fried Zucchini and their Flowers

SERVES 6

2 eggs, beaten
¾ cup all-purpose flour
1 cup milk
salt
18 zucchini flowers with about 2 inches of
zucchini still attached, washed and dried
carefully
oil for deep frying

Mix the eggs, flour, milk, and salt to taste together to make a smooth batter. Dip the flowers into the batter to coat them completely. Heat a large pan of oil until a small piece of bread dropped into it sizzles instantly. Fry the zucchini flowers about 30 seconds until crisp and golden brown. Drain on paper towels and sprinkle with salt. Serve hot.

Deep fry the zucchini flowers in sizzling hot oil about 30 seconds (below left).

FIORI DI ZUCCHINE (below), *with cherries as a colorful decorative touch.*

CRESPELLE DI RICOTTA E SPINACI

Ricotta and Spinach Crêpes

SERVES 6

Crêpes (makes 12)
½ cup all-purpose flour
⅞ cup milk
5 eggs
a pinch of salt
5 tablespoons butter, melted and cooled
butter or oil for cooking

Filling
½ lb (1 cup) ricotta cheese
½ cup chopped cooked spinach
2 cloves garlic finely chopped
1 tablespoon chopped fresh parsley
1 tablespoon chopped fresh basil
½ cup freshly grated Parmesan cheese
1 tablespoon olive oil
salt and freshly ground black pepper

Béchamel Sauce
2 tablespoons butter
5 tablespoons all-purpose flour
2 cups milk
a pinch of grated nutmeg
a pinch of salt
cheese to taste

To Finish
2 tablespoons freshly grated Parmesan cheese
2 tablespoons dried bread crumbs
2 tablespoons butter, cubed

First make the crêpes. Beat the flour and milk together until smooth, then beat in the eggs, salt, and butter. Stir very thoroughly until the mixture is completely amalgamated and free of lumps. Let it rest 30 minutes.

In a 7-inch crêpe pan or skillet, heat about ½ teaspoon of fat, making sure the pan is evenly coated. Stir the batter thoroughly, then pour in just enough to coat the pan evenly. Shake gently and cook about 1 minute or until the crêpe is like paper and just golden on the bottom. Turn over and cook 1 minute on the other side. Turn out onto a plate. Stack the crêpes interleaved with paper towel.

Mix together the filling ingredients and season to taste. Fill the crêpes and fold them into triangles. Arrange them, overlapping slightly, in an ovenproof dish.

To make the béchamel, melt the butter in a heavy-bottomed saucepan until foaming. Add the flour and stir to make a smooth paste which comes away from the sides of the pan.

Meanwhile, heat the milk until just below boiling point. Remove the saucepan with the flour and butter from the heat and gradually stir in the hot milk. Once all the milk has been added, use a whisk to blend the ingredients thoroughly. Return to the heat and continue to cook, stirring constantly with a wooden spoon, until the sauce no longer tastes of flour (about 5 minutes). Stir in the nutmeg and salt and remove from the heat. Add the cheese and return it to the heat for a couple of minutes.

Pour the sauce over the crêpes. Sprinkle with cheese and bread crumbs and dot with the butter. Bake in a moderate oven (350°F) 20–25 minutes or until golden brown. Serve hot.

CRESPELLE DI RICOTTA E SPINACI (left)
MILANESE STREET (right)

66

MOZZARELLA IN CARROZZA

Deep-Fried Mozzarella

SERVES 6

12 slices of white bread, crusts removed
1 cup milk (more may be required)
1 lb mozzarella cheese, sliced
dried oregano
¾ cup all-purpose flour
3 eggs, beaten
salt and freshly ground pepper
dried bread crumbs
oil for deep frying
lettuce, to serve

Dip one side of each slice of bread quickly in the milk, then lay a slice of mozzarella on the dry side of 6 of the slices. Sprinkle the mozzarella with dried oregano and cover with the other 6 slices of bread, dry side inward, to make sandwiches. Coat the sandwiches in flour, then in the beaten egg which should be seasoned with salt and pepper, and finally in bread crumbs. Make sure the sides of the "sandwiches" are well sealed.

Heat a large pan of oil until a small piece of bread dropped into it sizzles instantly. Fry the sandwiches one or two at a time until crisp. Drain on paper towels, cut into triangles, and serve hot on a bed of lettuce.

STREET MARKET *Because the Milanese expect such high quality in their food and drink, both expensive specialist shops and ordinary markets alike have high standards to meet.*

FICHI VERDI CON ZABAGLIONE DI PROSECCO

Green Figs with Prosecco Zabaglione

SERVES 6

12 ripe green figs
4 egg yolks
¼ cup caster sugar
4 tablespoons Prosecco or other sparkling white wine

Slice all the figs in half lengthwise. Put the egg yolks, sugar, and wine in the top half of a double boiler or in a heatproof bowl placed over a pan of hot water. Beat over water that is kept just below boiling point until fluffy, light, and thickened (about 25 minutes).

Cover 6 large plates with the Zabaglione, arrange the cut figs in the middle – 4 half figs on each plate – and chill them until required or serve immediately.

DESIGNER DISHES *Appearances count in Milan – this is after all the home of Italy's best known nouvelle cuisine restaurant – and food is expected to look as good as it tastes.*

MANGIARE IN SPIAGGIA

Eating on the Beach

I am not a great lover of picnic tables and chairs; indeed, they are rarely used for Italian picnics. The exception, however, is for food eaten on the beach. There are few things I find more revolting than grains of sand crunching between one's back teeth – not to mention the amount of work that has gone into preparing food which then becomes inedible. So if we are having lunch on the beach, I always choose a site with tables and chairs, and food that can easily be eaten with the fingers. The only exception in this menu is the *panzanella*, which needs bowls and forks. Everything else can be packed before you set off, then just picked up and eaten.

Most Italian beaches are in fact very well equipped for people wanting to have lunch there. Although many have restaurants of their own, quite often there will be rough wooden tables and chairs set in shady places for those who wish to eat their own food.

You can usually buy drinks from the beach bar, and they will be happy to supply extra forks or plates or whatever you might have forgotten to pack. Many beaches even have a small table next to the brightly colored beach umbrella and deck chairs which you are invariably able to hire.

When I was younger and more adventurous, we used to have picnics at Cinqueterre. The Cinqueterre is an area near La Spezia in Liguria, made up of five fisher-men's villages which cling precariously to the cliff face and are difficult to get to by land. Here we would picnic not on the usual beaches but in sandy coves that could only be reached by boat. Our boatman was called Guelfo and he would row us out and around the furthermost point in his old wooden boat. When the boat drew level with the appointed spot he would drop anchor and wait while we inflated a small dinghy, into which the picnic and assorted oddments such as suntan oil and footballs would be placed. With flippers on our feet we would then swim in to shore, pushing the dinghy ahead of us with our hands and beaching it on the soft sand. At sunset, after we had enjoyed a wonderfully private day on "our" beach, we would be collected by Guelfo in the same way. I think I'll have to wait until my children are a little older before I take them on such an adventurous expedition.

Menu

Focaccia con Peperoni

Cotolette di Tacchino

Sedano con il Gorgonzola

Torta Salata

La Panzanella

Albicocche Ripiene di Ricotta e Noci

ALBICOCCHE RIPIENE DI RICOTTA E NOCI (right)

LUNCH BY THE SEA (right) *Shaded tables and chairs are provided on many Italian beaches so you can eat in comfort.*

FOCACCIA CON PEPERONI

Focaccia with Braised Peppers

SERVES *6*

You can buy focaccia ready-made in most specialty food shops. If you wish, substitute some very crusty bread or pita for the focaccia.

6 squares or rectangles of focaccia, each about 8 inches square
3 large, fleshy sweet peppers, any color
4 tablespoons olive oil
2 cloves garlic, chopped
salt and freshly ground pepper
butter (optional)

Split each piece of focaccia open to make an envelope. Wash and dry the peppers, cut them in half, and remove all seeds and membranes. Slice them into strips. Heat the oil and the garlic together about 3 minutes, then add the peppers. Stir, then cover and allow to braise gently about 15 minutes or until soft. Season well. Stir occasionally and add water if necessary.

If the beach is very near, you can put the peppers into the bread envelopes while still warm; otherwise wait until they're completely cold to prevent the bread getting really soggy. If you like, you can spread the bread with butter before filling.

Focaccia is obviously a very convenient picnic bread and can be filled with a huge variety of different fillings. Slices of mozzarella and tomato, prosciutto, or cooked mixed vegetables are just a few other suggestions.

COTOLETTE DI TACCHINO

Turkey Cutlets

SERVES *6*

12 very thin slices of turkey breast, or 12 small turkey cutlets
2 eggs, beaten
salt and freshly ground pepper
3 cups fresh bread crumbs
oil for frying
lemon wedges

Flatten the turkey slices or cutlets as much as possible with a meat pounder. Put the turkey in the beaten egg, season with salt and pepper, and let it rest about 1 hour.

Remove the turkey from the egg and let any excess egg drip off, then smother each slice generously in bread crumbs. Heat 2 inches of oil until sizzling and fry all the cutlets until golden brown. They will need about 2 minutes on each side. Drain very thoroughly on paper towels.

Serve cold, with lemon wedges to squeeze over them.

FOCACCIA CON PEPERONI

72

SEDANO CON IL GORGONZOLA

Celery with Gorgonzola

SERVES 6

¼ lb gorgonzola cheese
½ lb (1 cup) ricotta cheese
2 tablespoons milk (more may be necessary)
1 small onion, finely chopped
a pinch of paprika
salt
2 tablespoons olive oil
2 sprigs celery leaves, finely chopped
12 stalks celery, each cut into 3 sections

Put the gorgonzola into a food processor or blender with the ricotta, milk, chopped onion, paprika, and salt to taste. Whizz until blended, then add the oil and the celery leaves.

Wash the celery pieces carefully and make sure they are properly dry. Fill with the cheese mixture and chill until required.

TORTA SALATA

Savory Pie

SERVES 6

Pastry
2 cups all-purpose flour
10 tablespoons (1¼ sticks) butter or margarine,
softened
1 egg
cold water to mix
salt
Filling
¾ lb (1½ cups) ricotta cheese
½ lb fontina or Edam cheese, freshly grated
1 stick of butter or margarine, softened
5 eggs, separated

Sift the flour onto the work top in a pile and plunge your fist into the center to make a hole; put the remaining pastry ingredients into this hole. Blend together quickly with your fingertips to make a soft, elastic ball of dough. Try not to knead the dough as this will make it heavy. Cover with a cloth and put in a cool place to rest 1 hour.

Meanwhile, press the ricotta through a sieve into a bowl. Add the grated cheese, butter and 5 egg yolks and mix lightly but thoroughly to create an even texture. Beat the egg whites until stiff and fold into the ricotta mixture.

Butter a 9-inch tart pan and dust with flour. Roll out three-quarters of the pastry and use to line the pan. Fill it with the ricotta mixture. Roll out the rest of the pastry, cut into strips, and use to make a lattice on top.

Bake in a preheated moderately hot oven (375°F) about 40 minutes or until set and golden brown. Serve cold or just warm.

LA PANZANELLA

Tomato and Bread Salad

SERVES 6

4 large Marmande or other flavorful tomatoes,
cut into wedges
2 large onions, finely sliced
1 hothouse cucumber, peeled and cut into cubes
a handful of fresh basil leaves
3 stale white bread rolls, soaked in cold water about
1 hour
about 6 tablespoons olive oil
3 tablespoons white wine vinegar
salt and freshly ground pepper

Put the tomatoes and onions into a bowl with the cucumber and basil leaves. Mix together with your hands. Take the bread out of the water, squeeze it dry with your hands, and mix into the salad. Dress with plenty of olive oil, vinegar, and salt and pepper to taste. Toss it all together and let stand at least 2 hours. It is even better if left overnight in the refrigerator.

ALBICOCCHE RIPIENE DI RICOTTA E NOCI

Apricots with Almond and Ricotta Filling

SERVES 6

about 24 almonds
½ lb (1 cup) ricotta cheese
a pinch of ground cinnamon
2 tablespoons sugar
12 fresh apricots, carefully pitted but left as intact as
possible

Peel and chop finely 12 of the almonds. Mash the ricotta carefully and stir in the cinnamon, chopped almonds, and sugar. Fill each apricot carefully with this mixture, then decorate each one with a whole almond and chill until required.

Fresh dates are also very good when stuffed with this filling. A further variation is to substitute walnuts for the almonds.

TORTA SALATA (left)

ALBICOCCHE RIPIENE DI RICOTTA E NOCI (right)

L'ANNIVERSARIO DI NOZZE

Wedding Anniversary Dinner

My brother Howard and his wife, Benedetta, are the ultimate childhood sweethearts, so their twelfth wedding anniversary was a very special occasion. We decided to hold their anniversary dinner in their favorite restaurant, tucked away in the backstreets of central Milan behind La Scala.

The restaurant looks totally anonymous from the outside and the sign bears no name, just the word Trattoria. Yet once inside you discover the atmosphere of a well-established and serious eating house, the walls decorated with framed napkins upon which the many famous names who have eaten here have either drawn or written a few words.

As the owner is Tuscan, the food has a light and rustic style about it that is light years away from the more heavy-duty Lombard cuisine. Milan, in fact, offers the very best of any regional or international food, if you know where to find it. My brother and his wife are both excellent cooks and fairly passionate gourmets, so one is always guaranteed very good food in their company! This evening turned out to be no exception – they invited all their closest friends to join them for what proved to be a memorable anniversary banquet.

We began with *capesante gratinate*, a dish of scallops coated with a piquant and delicious grilled topping of anchovies, capers, garlic, and bread crumbs, with the unusual addition of chopped pickled onions for a truly unique flavor. To follow there were *crostini alla Toscana*, toasted Tuscan bread covered with a purée of ground beef and chicken liver. We moved from the antipasti to the first courses – a spectacular seafood spaghetti dish, *spaghetti allo scoglio*, which looked so attractive with many of the shellfish left in their shells, and a light and delicate risotto with zucchini and their flowers.

The next course, *tagliata vegetariana*, looked as good as it tasted. A large platter of paper-thin slices of beef tenderloin was covered with a selection of vegetables and it was the many different tastes and textures of the dish which made it especially interesting.

The masterpiece of the evening had to be the enormous sea bass, baked in a covering of rock salt and egg white so that it was as brown on the outside as a loaf of well-baked bread. When the salt crust was split open you could virtually smell the sea as the aroma of the fish, cooked without condiments of any kind, filtered through the cracks. Anyone who had thought they couldn't possibly eat any more needed no further persuasion!

At this point a multi-colored, multi-flavored salad with a delicious dressing was served, and it was perfect for clearing the way for Franco's dessert specialty: the most wonderfully rich, gooey *tiramisù* I have ever eaten, made with the freshest mascarpone. The lightest possible end to this really superb meal was provided with tiny *fragoline al vino bianco*, wonderful wild strawberries soaked in white wine Wild strawberries are actually quite common in Italy and they were a delicious finishing touch to linger over before over *espressos*. We rolled out into the balmy night, feeling replete and knowing we had celebrated the wedding anniversary in the best possible style.

MILAN TRATTORIA *The restaurant where we held Howard and Benedetta's dinner is a real haven, comfortable yet with a serious attitude to the food it serves. We arrived fairly early, as the staff were finishing their own meal.*

Menu

Capesante Gratinate

Crostini alla Toscana

Spaghetti allo Scoglio

Risotto con Zucchine e Fiori

Tagliata Vegetariana

Branzino al Sale

Tiramisù

Fragoline al Vino Bianco

CAPESANTE GRATINATE

Gratin of Scallops

SERVES 6

18 sea scallops, cleaned and ready to cook
⅓ cup fresh bread crumbs
3 tablespoons chopped fresh parsley
2 tablespoons capers, rinsed, dried, and chopped
3 canned anchovies, rinsed, dried, and chopped
2 cloves garlic, chopped
3 small pickled onions, rinsed, dried, and chopped
½ cup olive oil

Lay the scallops, in their half shells, in a flat ovenproof dish. Mix the bread crumbs with the parsley, capers, anchovies, garlic, and pickled onions in a bowl. Add the oil and stir until well mixed. Cover each scallop with a good spoonful of this paste. Place in a preheated moderately hot oven (400°F), and bake about 15–20 minutes, depending on the size of the scallops, or until crisp on the top. Take care not to overcook them or they will be rubbery. Serve hot.

GARLIC FOR SALE *Straw baskets overflow with freshly picked garlic on this rudimentary market stall in Milan.*

CROSTINI ALLA TOSCANA

Tuscan Toast

SERVES 6

2 cloves garlic, chopped
1 small onion, chopped
3 sprigs of fresh parsley, chopped
4 tablespoons olive oil
¼ lb lean beef steak, ground
¼ lb chicken livers, ground
½ wineglass of dry red wine
½ wineglass of red wine vinegar
1 tablespoon tomato paste
⅔ cup stock or broth
salt and freshly ground pepper
2 tablespoons capers, rinsed, drained, and chopped
3 canned anchovies, rinsed, drained, and chopped, or 1 heaped tablespoon anchovy paste
thin slices of French or Italian bread, toasted, to serve

Fry the garlic, onion, and parsley together gently in the olive oil until the onion is soft. Add the ground beef and chicken livers and cook until well browned and crumbly.

Pour on the wine and boil to evaporate the alcohol fumes 2 or 3 minutes. Add the vinegar and boil to evaporate the fumes in the same way. Add the tomato paste and stir carefully. Cook 8–10 minutes, stirring the mixture occasionally.

Stir in the stock and seasoning. Cover and simmer 1 hour. Ten minutes before serving, stir in the chopped capers and anchovies or anchovy paste.

To serve, spread the mixture on toasted slices of French or Italian bread.

FRESHLY CAUGHT CLAMS *When serving clams in their shells, make sure you scrub the outside and rinse them thoroughly before using.*

SPAGHETTI ALLO SCOGLIO

SPAGHETTI ALLO SCOGLIO

Reef Spaghetti

Ready cooked, fresh shellfish may be used in this dish, but they will need less time to cook.

SERVES 6

5 tablespoons olive oil
3 cloves garlic, finely chopped
2¼ lb mixed shellfish such as clams, mussels, scallops, etc., including shells, washed and cleaned
salt and freshly ground pepper
1 large wineglass of white wine
2 tablespoons tomato paste
1 lb spaghetti
3 tablespoons chopped fresh parsley

Heat the oil in a large pan with the garlic until the garlic is golden brown. Season with salt and pepper, then pour in the wine and stir again. Allow the alcohol from the wine to evaporate 2 or 3 minutes, then add the tomato paste and stir again. Remove the scallops from their shells if necessary, then toss in all the shellfish (which must be scrupulously clean and sand- or grit-free) and mix together thoroughly. Remove from the heat as soon as all the shells have opened up.

Bring a large pot of salted water to a boil, toss in the spaghetti, and stir. Cook until the spaghetti is *al dente* then drain immediately and transfer the spaghetti to the pan with the shellfish. Return to the heat and toss to mix everything together 2–3 minutes. Sprinkle with parsley and serve at once.

RISOTTO CON ZUCCHINE E FIORI

Risotto with Zucchini and their Flowers

SERVES 6

1½ quarts vegetable or chicken stock
7 young, tender zucchini, with their flowers if
possible
4 tablespoons olive oil
salt and freshly ground pepper
2 cups risotto (arborio) rice
1 tablespoon unsalted butter
⅓ cup freshly grated Parmesan cheese

Heat the stock to just below boiling point. Meanwhile, slice the zucchini and their flowers very finely. In a large deep skillet or wide saucepan, fry the sliced zucchini and flowers until tender in the olive oil. Add the rice and stir it to coat with the oil. Season, then begin to add the hot stock, stirring constantly to prevent sticking. Never add more than one ladleful of liquid at a time and wait for the rice to absorb it before adding any more. (You may not need all the liquid, depending on the quality of the rice.) The rice will take 20 minutes to cook from the time you begin adding the liquid.

Remove from the heat. Adjust the seasoning, stir in the butter and cheese, and transfer to a platter to serve.

ZUCCHINI FLOWERS (left) *The vibrant orange of zucchini flowers makes them as attractive to look at as to eat.*

SAUTÉED ARTICHOKES *Artichokes, either on their own or mixed with other vegetables, taste particularly good in* tagliata vegetariana.

TAGLIATA VEGETARIANA

Thinly Sliced Beef Tenderloin with Mixed Vegetables

SERVES 6

1 beef tenderloin roast, weighing about 1¾ lb
3–4 tablespoons olive oil
salt
freshly ground pepper
about 1 lb mixed vegetables cooked separately,
such as sautéed artichokes, grilled radicchio,
steamed asparagus, sautéed mushrooms, etc.,
kept warm
(you can have a mixture of vegetables or only one
type if you prefer)

Slice the tenderloin as thinly as possible using a very sharp knife (or you could ask your butcher to do this for you). Grease a flat ovenproof dish lightly with a little of the oil, then arrange the meat slices on top in rows, slightly overlapping. Sprinkle the meat with the remaining oil and with salt and freshly ground pepper to taste.

Place in a preheated moderately hot oven (400°F) and roast about 3 minutes just to seal the meat. This will leave the meat very pink. If you like your meat medium rare, then roast it 4–5 minutes.

Remove from the oven, cover with all the vegetables to hide the meat completely, and serve at once.

An alternative is to serve the cooked mixed vegetables cold with the warm meat. The different textures make an interesting and delicious contrast.

Clean the fish carefully and dry both inside and out with paper towel.
To cook the fish you will need a large baking dish lined with foil.

BRANZINO AL SALE

Sea Bass Baked in Salt

Gray mullet makes a good alternative to sea bass.

SERVES 6

1 fresh sea bass, weighing about 3¼ lb, drawn
3¼ lb (about 8½ cups) fine sea salt
5 egg whites
For serving
olive oil
lemon wedges

Wash the fish carefully. Dry it all over, inside and out, with paper towels, then lay it in a baking dish lined with foil (cut off the head if it does not fit in the dish).

Mix the salt with the egg whites until you have a smooth, even texture. Cover the fish completely and thickly with the salt mixture. Bake in a preheated moderately hot oven (375°F) about 40 minutes. When it is ready, it should look like a well-baked loaf of bread.

To serve, break the crust of salt along both sides with a very sharp knife and lift off the top. Lift the fish onto a serving platter and divide into portions. Serve with a little jug of olive oil and some lemon wedges.

Other fish can be cooked in this way, too, as long as they have a thick scaly skin. Mullet and porgy are suitable alternatives.

THE PIÈCE DE RÉSISTANCE *The real high point of the meal was the spectacular* branzino al sale, *or sea bass in its crusty coating of sea salt.*

TIRAMISÙ

Pick Me Up

SERVES 8–10

1 lb mascarpone or rich cream cheese
8 eggs, separated
½ cup sugar
½ cup very strong espresso coffee
1¼ cups weak coffee
⅓ cup brandy
about 30 ladyfinger cookies
ground coffee or cocoa powder for dusting

Beat the mascarpone or cream cheese with a wooden spoon to make it soft and creamy. Beat the egg yolks in a separate bowl until fluffy and pale yellow. Add the sugar to the egg yolks a little at a time until you have a smooth texture, then add this to the cream cheese mixture. Stir in the strong coffee. Beat the egg whites separately until stiff, then fold them into the cheese, egg, and coffee mixture. Set this mixture aside.

Pour the weak coffee and brandy into a bowl. Dip the ladyfingers into it one at a time, to moisten them, and arrange the cookies in a layer in the bottom of a shallow bowl. Cover with some of the cheese mixture, then cover with more moistened cookies. Continue to make layers in this way until you have used up all the ingredients, ending with a layer of cheese mixture. Sprinkle with the ground coffee or cocoa powder and chill at least 1 hour or until required.

After beating the mascarpone to a soft, creamy texture, beat the eggs in a separate bowl. Once they are fluffy and pale yellow, add the sugar to them.

In a shallow dish, make alternate layers of moistened ladyfingers and cheese mixture.

FRAGOLINE AL VINO BIANCO

Wild Strawberries with White Wine

SERVES 6

1 lb (2 pints) wild or alpine strawberries (or ordinary strawberries cut into small pieces)
3 tablespoons sugar
1 wineglass of dry white wine (even better if it's champagne!)

Hull and wash the strawberries carefully. Dry them and arrange them in a bowl. Sprinkle over the sugar and pour the wine over them. Leave to macerate in the refrigerator about 2 hours before serving.

Raspberries are also delicious when soaked in wine, particularly a sparkling dry white wine like Italian Prosecco. Prepare them in the same way as strawberries.

Another alternative is the interesting contrast of a sour fruit, such as medlar or citrus fruit, soaked in a sweet white wine such as Asti Spumante.

LA FESTA DELLA RICOTTA

A Feast of Ricotta

I can remember how fascinated I was when I was first taken up into the mountains to watch the shepherds making ricotta. Nowadays most ricotta is made from cow's milk as opposed to the original version which was made exclusively from ewe's milk. It is a very soft, fresh cheese which is used a great deal in Italian cooking both in sweet and savory dishes, as well as being eaten on its own sprinkled with sugar or cinnamon. As a little girl, my typical *merenda*, or tea-time snack, would be a huge slab of bread covered with ricotta and then coated with sugar.

Ricotta is a particularly good partner for fresh spinach and mashed together in *gnocchi* these two ingredients make a wonderful combination. It also crops up in pies, pasta, on pizzas, and in savory turnovers. If Parmesan cheese is the king of Italian cheeses, then ricotta has to be the queen.

Ricotta forms the basis of the most famous of all Sicilian desserts: *la cassata*. Although this has now become the name for an international ice cream, the original dish is a cake so rich and overpoweringly filling that it

FLOCK OF SHEEP (left) *Traditionally, ricotta is made from ewe's milk, although nowadays most of the ricotta on sale is made with milk from cows.*

could not be from anywhere but Sicily. It is actually fairly simple to make – a casing of sponge cake is filled with a creamy ricotta filling, then decorated with a sumptuously thick frosting and

candied fruits. Historically, cassata was made by nuns in celebration of Easter, but in time they had to be forbidden from making it because they were neglecting their holy duties for cake making.

Nowadays there seems to be no particular time of year to eat cassata, and in Sicily you will be offered it constantly.

The other superb cakes made with ricotta in Sicily are the lovely *cannoli alla Siciliana*. To make these pastries you need a special Sicilian kit of metal or bamboo tubes to keep them perfectly hollow and in shape. The filling – ricotta with icing sugar and candied peel – is incredibly sweet.

If you ever get a chance to taste ricotta that has only just been made and is therefore still warm, you will discover a cheese that is very different indeed from the plastic-wrapped supermarket variety – and you'll be hooked!

Menu

Cannelloni Ripieni di Ricotta e Salsicce

Culigiones

Calzone

Ricotta in Canape

Budino di Ricotta

Crostata di Ricotta

Cassata alla Siciliana

MAKING RICOTTA (left) *The ricotta-making process varies slightly from region to region, and one can also find salted and smoked versions of the cheese.*

TRADITIONAL RICOTTA PRODUCTION *The word "ricotta," which literally means "re-cooked," derives from the process by which the cheese is made. First of all, the milk is heated (above and above right) until the whey separates. (Often the curd is used to produce other cheeses.) The whey is then skimmed off and reheated to a high temperature, at which point thicker lumps of whey begin to form on the surface. It is this thickened whey which is in turn skimmed off and put in the traditional wicker baskets which allow it to drain (right). The finished cheese is never aged but is eaten or used fresh. Molise is famous for its top quality cheese, but there are also many other areas in the country producing excellent ricotta.*

CANNELLONI RIPIENI DI RICOTTA E SALSICCE

Cannelloni with a Ricotta and Sausage Filling

SERVES 6

Pasta
1¾ cups all-purpose flour
a pinch of salt
3 eggs
2–3 tablespoons water

Tomato Sauce
3 tablespoons butter or olive oil
1 clove garlic, finely chopped
1 small onion, finely chopped
1 small carrot, finely chopped
1 small stalk celery, finely chopped
3 tablespoons tomato paste
1 cup water
salt and freshly ground pepper

Filling
3 large Italian sausages
1 lb (2 cups) ricotta cheese
a pinch of salt
1 egg, beaten
⅓ cup freshly grated Parmesan cheese

To Finish
butter for greasing
⅓ cup freshly grated Parmesan cheese
3 tablespoons butter, cubed

Make the pasta first. Sift the flour and salt onto the work top in a pile and push your fist into the center to make a hole. Put the eggs and water into the hole. Knead all these together very thoroughly. You can also do this in the food processor. Begin to roll out the dough, then fold it in half and roll out again. Continue to do this until it is smooth and elastic and you hear the air pop out from under the fold as you press down with the rolling pin. Cover the dough with a cloth and put it to one side.

To make the sauce, heat the butter or oil in a saucepan and fry the garlic, onion, carrot, and celery until the vegetables are completely soft. Add the tomato paste and water, stir, and season to taste. Simmer the tomato sauce gently about 20–30 minutes.

Put the sausages in a skillet, prick them all over, and cover with cold water. Cook over a low heat until the water has evaporated, then sizzle the sausages in their own fat 5 or 6 minutes. Remove from the pan and allow them to cool.

Meanwhile, make the filling. Press the ricotta through a sieve, into a bowl, and add the salt, egg, and grated Parmesan. Stir everything thoroughly. Skin the sausages and crumble the meat into the ricotta mixture. Stir it all together.

Roll out the pasta dough to a thickness of about 1/10 inch and cut into 3 inch squares. Bring a very large pot of salted water to a boil and cook the squares 4 at a time about 1 minute or until they rise to the surface. Scoop the squares out with a slotted spoon as soon as they are ready and lay them on the work top or on wet dish towels.

Butter an ovenproof dish carefully. Fill each pasta square with ricotta filling, roll closed, and lay them in rows in the ovenproof dish. Sprinkle over the grated Parmesan, scatter on the cubes of butter, and pour the tomato sauce all over to cover. Bake the cannelloni in a preheated moderately hot oven (375°F) about 30 minutes. Serve hot.

CULIGIONES

Sardinian Ravioli

SERVES 6

Pasta
3½ cups all-purpose flour
5 eggs
½ teaspoon oil, for oiling rolling pin
Filling
½ cup fresh ricotta cheese
2 large potatoes, peeled, boiled, and mashed
⅓ cup freshly grated Parmesan cheese
3 tablespoons freshly grated Romano cheese or hard
goat's cheese
2 tablespoons chopped fresh mixed herbs
salt and freshly ground pepper
5 tablespoons unsalted butter, melted, to serve

Make the pasta first as on page 87, but without adding any salt or water. Roll out the dough until it is elastic and as thin as possible. (Rub the oil on the rolling pin to help you roll.)

Cut the pasta into 24 squares, each about 4 inches on each side. Cover with a cloth while you quickly prepare the filling.

Press the ricotta through a sieve into a bowl and mix it with the potatoes, cheeses, and herbs. Season with salt and pepper.

Place about 1 tablespoon filling on 12 of the pasta squares and cover with the other 12 squares. Press the edges closed securely to seal the filling inside.

Bring a large pot of salted water to a rolling boil and slip the squares into the water. Cook 4–5 minutes, then remove with a slotted spatula. Arrange 2 ravioli on each of 6 warm plates. Cover each portion with melted butter and serve at once.

CALZONE

Stuffed pizza

SERVES *6*

Dough
2⅓ *cups all-purpose flour*
½ *oz fresh compressed yeast*
1¼ *cups warm water*
a pinch of sugar
2 tablespoons olive oil
a pinch of salt
oil for greasing
Filling
10 canned anchovy fillets, drained
6 sun-dried tomatoes
½ *lb (1 cup) ricotta cheese*

Pile the flour on the work top and push your fist into the center to make a hole. Crumble the yeast into the center and add the sugar. Using a fork, blend enough water into the yeast to make a smooth paste. Then gradually add more water as necessary and knead the flour, yeast, and sugar mixture together very thoroughly with your hands. About halfway through the kneading, add the salt and oil.

Continue to knead the dough until it is smooth and elastic. Then place the ball of dough in a lightly floured bowl and cover it with a lightly floured cloth. Let rise in a warm spot about 2½ hours, when it should have doubled in volume.

CALZONE (left)

Meanwhile, make the filling. Rinse the anchovy fillets, then chop the anchovies and the tomatoes into small pieces and mix with the ricotta. Set aside until required.

When the dough has doubled in volume, remove it from the bowl and divide it into 6 pieces. Flatten each piece into a disk shape about ¼ inch thick. Place filling in the middle of the dough, then fold the dough in half and seal the edges carefully with your fingers. Place the *calzone* on an oiled baking sheet and bake in a preheated hot oven (400°F) 20 minutes or until golden brown. Brush the surface with olive oil and serve hot.

RICOTTA IN CANAPE

Ricotta with Eggs

SERVES *6*

1 lb (2 cups) ricotta cheese; cut into 6 slices
4 tablespoons butter
6 eggs
6 tablespoons puréed tomatoes
a large pinch of dried mixed herbs
salt and freshly ground pepper
6 tablespoons freshly grated Parmesan or other cheese

Fry the slices of ricotta in the butter until just browned on both sides. Lay them in an ovenproof dish. Break the eggs on top and cover with the puréed tomatoes. Sprinkle with the herbs, salt and pepper to taste, and grated Parmesan. Bake in a preheated moderately hot oven (400°F) 15 minutes or until the eggs have set. Serve hot.

BUDINO DI RICOTTA

Ricotta Pudding

SERVES *6*

1¼ *cups cold water*
⅓ *cup semolina*
14 oz (1¾ cups) fresh ricotta cheese
¼ *cup granulated or confectioners' sugar*
1 egg
1 egg yolk
1 heaped tablespoon chopped mixed candied peel
1 heaped tablespoon golden raisins
1–2 tablespoons dark rum
1 egg white
butter for greasing
a handful of dried bread crumbs or semolina
¼ *cup confectioners' sugar, to finish*

Bring the water to a boil, then sprinkle in the semolina very slowly, stirring constantly to prevent lumps. It will thicken very quickly. When it is thick and smooth, remove from the heat and tip into a bowl. Let cool.

Mash the ricotta with the sugar, egg, egg yolk, candied peel, raisins, and rum. Blend in the semolina. Beat the egg white until stiff and fold it into the mixture.

Butter a 6-cup soufflé dish thoroughly and coat it carefully with bread crumbs or semolina. Tip it upside-down to remove the loose crumbs. Pour the ricotta mixture into the dish, making sure it comes no more than two-thirds of the way up the sides.

Bake in a preheated moderate oven (350°F) 45 minutes–1 hour or until golden brown. Unmold the pudding onto a platter. Cover with sifted confectioners' sugar and serve warm or cold.

CROSTATA DI RICOTTA

Ricotta Tart

SERVES *6*

Pastry
1½ cups all-purpose flour
¼ cup cornstarch
2½ tablespoons confectioners' sugar
10 tablespoons (1¼ sticks) unsalted butter
grated rind of 1 lemon
Custard
2 tablespoons sugar
2 egg yolks
1 tablespoon all-purpose flour
1¼ cups milk
Filling
¾ lb (1½ cups) ricotta cheese
3 eggs, separated
3 tablespoons sugar
a large pinch of ground cinnamon
3 tablespoons chopped mixed candied peel
To Finish
butter for greasing
1 egg, beaten
¼ cup vanilla-flavored sugar

Make the pastry. Sift the flour, cornstarch and confectioners' sugar into a bowl and add the butter and lemon rind. Blend everything together quickly with your fingertips or a pastry blender to make a smooth, light dough. Don't knead it or it will be heavy. Add a little water if necessary. Let rest under a cloth about 30 minutes.

Next make the custard. Mix the sugar, egg yolks, and flour together in a heavy-bottomed saucepan until completely smooth. Add the milk and place over the heat. Cook, stirring constantly, until the custard thickens and coats the back of the spoon. Cool.

For the filling, mix the ricotta in a bowl with the egg yolks, sugar, cinnamon, and peel. Stir in the cooled custard. Beat the egg whites until stiff and fold into the mixture.

Roll out about two-thirds of the pastry and use to line a buttered tart pan with a removable base (or a flan ring placed on a baking sheet). Pour the ricotta filling into the pastry case. Roll out the remaining pastry, cut it into strips, and lay over the filling to make a lattice. Brush the pastry with beaten egg.

Bake in a preheated moderate oven (350°F) about 35 minutes or until golden brown. When the tart is baked, remove it from the pan and let it cool. Dust the top of the tart with vanilla-flavored sugar just before serving.

CASSATA ALLA SICILIANA (opposite, left) *and* CANNOLI ALLA SICILIANA (opposite, right) *The latter are delicious little pastries with a rich filling of ricotta and candied orange peel.*

CASSATA ALLA SICILIANA

Sicilian Cassata Cake

SERVES *6*

1¼ lb (2½ cups) fresh ricotta cheese
2 cups confectioners' sugar, sifted
1 teaspoon vanilla extract
4 tablespoons maraschino liqueur
¼ cup finely chopped semisweet chocolate
¼ cup chopped mixed candied fruit
10 oz sponge cake, thinly sliced
To decorate
assorted candied fruits
Icing
1 cup confectioners' sugar, sifted
1–2 tablespoons cold water
2 tablespoons maraschino liqueur

Press the ricotta through a sieve into a bowl and beat in the confectioners' sugar and vanilla extract to make a smooth, light, and fluffy texture. Stir in the liqueur, chocolate, and candied fruit.

Use the cake slices to line the sides and bottom of a 6-inch cake pan, using some of the ricotta mixture to help stick the cake to the pan if it slips. Put the ricotta cream into the lined cake pan, smooth the surface, and cover the top with more cake. Chill about 1 hour or until set slightly.

Unmold the cake onto a platter. To make the icing, mix the confectioners' sugar with enough water and the liqueur until silky smooth, then spread all over the cake. Chill again to set the icing. Decorate with candied fruit to serve. Chill until required.

NOZZE SICILIANE

A Wedding in Sicily

Give any Italian an excuse for celebrating and it's guaranteed that they will push the boat out. If they are Sicilian, you can bet whatever you like that they will do it more extravagantly and with more pomp and circumstance than any other Italian. A wedding has to be the very best reason for a celebration and the Sicilians certainly lived up to their reputation on the day Luisa and Marco were married in Palermo.

The wedding reception was held on the wide, Baroque terraces of Palermo's sumptuous Palazzo Butera. It was such an amazing setting for a wedding, with views over the roof tops of the city and the atmosphere of grandeur and elegance which the old *palazzi* always seem to impose. I was amazed at the smooth running of the operation – there were so many staff to organize, before one even thought about the guests or the bride and groom. Yet everything was elegantly color-coordinated, from the yellow and white tablecloths through to the parcels of sugared almonds wrapped in white tulle and decorated with tiny sprigs of yellow mimosa.

There were actually about fifty different things to eat and I have selected ten of my favorites for the menu here to give you a taste of the day. As well as all the food laid out on the buffet, there were three cooks/craftsmen who were stationed on the terrace to provide additional delicacies. They were the *poliparo* – the "octopus man" who prepared grilled octopus on a barbecue, as well as fish kebabs and other delicacies on request; the *friggitore*, or fryer, presided over a huge cauldron of boiling oil and fried all manner of fish and vegetables; the *focacciere* had the job of preparing pizzas and focaccia.

All Italians take their food very seriously, but at a wedding feast they really do throw all thought of calorie counting and cholesterol levels to the wind. If you are ever invited to an Italian wedding, the only strategy is simply to join in the general feeling of, "Oh, well, there's always tomorrow to recover," and just enjoy the day. The first time I attended a wedding was in the Abruzzi, in central Italy, where they really do these things properly. We began to eat at about midday and didn't actually get up from the table until well past seven o'clock in the evening. At this point we followed the happy, if extremely full, couple on foot back to the house where they were to spend their first wedding night, heckling them and throwing sugared almonds at them all the way there!

Luisa and Marco's wedding ended on a rather more sedate note, with an incredible sunset which painted the sky every shade of orange and red over the roofs of Palermo.

Menu

Sarde a Beccafico

Peperoni Arrosto

Melanzane Fritte in Insalata

Pesce alla Matalotta

*Pollo alla Cacciatora
con Melanzane*

Cazzilli

Cassata Gelata alla Siciliana

Spuma Gelata di Pesche

Gelatina di Mandorle

Granita di Caffè con Panna

WAITING IN THE WINGS (left) *An army of waiters took care of the large number of guests.*

CONFETTI OF SUGARED ALMONDS (left) *are given to guests by the bride and groom.*

SARDE A BECCAFICO

Sicilian Sardines with Oranges

SERVES 8

3¼ lb large fresh sardines
⅔ cup olive oil
4½ cups fresh bread crumbs
⅔ cup golden raisins, soaked in cold water
15 minutes
1 cup pine nuts
¼ cup chopped fresh parsley
grated rind of 1 orange
juice of 2 oranges
2 teaspoons anchovy paste
salt and freshly ground pepper
bay leaves
1 orange, thinly sliced

Open up the sardines and gut them, then pull out the spine from the tail end, taking the head of each fish with the spine. Wash the dressed fish carefully and pat dry.

Heat about two-thirds of the oil in a skillet until very hot and add all but 1 tablespoon of the bread crumbs. Brown carefully all over, then tip into a bowl. Add the drained raisins, the pine nuts, parsley, orange rind and juice, and anchovy paste. Season to taste. Mix all this together and use it to stuff the fish.

Oil an ovenproof dish and lay the stuffed fish in the dish, inserting a bay leaf between each one. Pour the remaining oil over the top and sprinkle over the reserved bread crumbs. Bake in a preheated moderate oven (350°F) 30 minutes. Serve hot or cold, garnished with the orange slices.

PEPERONI ARROSTO

Grilled Sweet Pepper Strips

SERVES 8

6 large, fleshy sweet peppers of assorted colors
⅔ cup olive oil
2 cloves garlic, very finely chopped
1 tablespoon chopped fresh parsley
salt
freshly ground pepper

Cut the peppers in half, carefully remove all the seeds and membranes, and cut the peppers into wide strips. Place the strips under a preheated broiler or in a grilling rack over a flame to soften and brown slightly on both sides (they can go a bit black if you like).

Lay the pepper strips in a wide platter and pour over the oil. Sprinkle with the chopped garlic and parsley and season generously with salt and pepper. Serve warm or cold.

PEPERONI ARROSTO (above), *with a simple dressing of olive oil.*

MELANZANE FRITTE IN INSALATA

Fried Eggplant Salad

SERVES 8

1¼–2 cups olive oil or vegetable oil
4 large eggplants, cut into finger-thick slices

Dressing
a large pinch of dried oregano
4 tablespoons red wine vinegar
5 tablespoons olive oil
salt and freshly ground pepper

Heat the oil in a large skillet until sizzling hot, then fry the eggplant slices until well browned and slightly crisp on both sides. Drain carefully on paper towels, then arrange on a large platter. Pour over the dressing. Leave at least 30 minutes before serving to allow the flavors to develop.

SARDE A BECCAFICO (left)

MELANZANE FRITTE IN INSALATA (left)

PESCE ALLA MATALOTTA

Fish Casserole with Olives

SERVES *8*

3¼ lb any firm-fleshed fish, drawn
1 large onion, thinly sliced
⅔ cup olive oil
3 cloves garlic, finely chopped
2 cups puréed tomatoes or 3 tablespoons tomato
paste diluted in 2 cups warm water
2 heaped tablespoons capers, rinsed and dried
1¼ cups green olives, halved and pitted
salt and freshly ground black pepper
a handful of fresh parsley, chopped
8 fresh basil leaves
a small handful of fresh celery leaves

Wash and dry the fish carefully. If they are small, leave them whole; if they are large, cut them into even chunks.

Fry the onion in the olive oil in a large pan until soft, then add the garlic, puréed tomatoes, capers, and olives. Season to taste. Stir the ingredients together, then add the fish and the herbs. Spoon the sauce all over the fish.

Cover and simmer very gently about 30 minutes without stirring again. Serve hot.

THE BARBECUE (left) *provided additional, piping-hot delicacies.*

BAROQUE SPLENDOR (right) *The grandeur of the Palazzo Butera provided a sumptuous backdrop.*

POLLO ALLA CACCIATORA CON MELANZANE

Chicken with Eggplant

SERVES *8*

4 large eggplants, cut into finger-thick slices
salt and freshly ground pepper
8 chicken quarters
4 tablespoons olive oil
3 cloves garlic, chopped
6 slices bacon or pancetta
1¼ cups dry white wine
16-oz can tomatoes, chopped
oil for deep frying
3 tablespoons chopped fresh parsley

Put the eggplant slices in a large colander and sprinkle generously with salt. Cover with a plate with a weight on top and let the eggplant drain in the sink 1–2 hours to remove all the bitter juices.

Meanwhile, trim the chicken quarters. Heat the olive oil in a large, wide pan and fry the chicken pieces quickly with the garlic and bacon or *pancetta*, to brown them all over. Pour the wine over the chicken and let evaporate about 3 minutes, then add the tomatoes. Stir together and season to taste. Cover and simmer about 35 minutes.

Wipe dry the eggplant slices carefully and deep fry them in hot oil until tender and golden brown. Drain on paper towels. Stir them into the chicken dish and cook a further 5–10 minutes. Transfer to a serving dish, sprinkle with the parsley, and serve.

CAZZILLI

Sicilian Potato Fritters

SERVES 8

2¼ lb potatoes suitable for mashing
2 oz cooked ham
a large handful of fresh parsley
4 tablespoons butter, softened
4 egg yolks
salt
2 oz caciocavallo or provolone cheese, cubed
½ cup freshly grated Romano cheese
3–6 tablespoons all-purpose flour
4 egg whites, beaten until fluffy
3–4 cups fresh bread crumbs
oil for deep frying

Put the unpeeled potatoes in a pan of cold water, bring to a boil, and cook for 30 minutes. While the potatoes are cooking, chop the ham and parsley together.

Drain the potatoes and peel them while they are still hot. Push them through a ricer into a clean saucepan to make a smooth purée. While the purée is still warm, stir the butter into the puréed potato. Allow it to cool, then stir in the egg yolks, mixing well. Season to taste with salt, and add the chopped ham and parsley and the cubed cheese. Stir in the pecorino, and adjust seasoning as required.

Shape the mixture into 14–16 cylinders with your hands. Coat the cylinders in flour, then in egg white and then in bread crumbs.

Heat a large pan of oil until a piece of bread dropped into it sizzles instantly. Deep fry the *cazzilli*, a few at a time, until golden and crisp. Drain and serve piping hot.

CASSATA GELATA ALLA SICILIANA

Ice Cream Cassata

SERVES 8

1–1½ pints best quality vanilla ice cream, soft enough to spread
1¼ cups whipping cream
⅓ cup sugar
½ cup chopped mixed candied fruit
½ cup chopped toasted almonds
2 squares semisweet chocolate, chopped

Line the sides and the bottom of a 1-quart bombe mold or pudding basin (preferably metal) with the ice cream. Make sure the center remains empty so you can fill it with the other ingredients. Place the mold in the freezer to harden the ice cream.

Whip the cream with the sugar, then fold in the candied fruit, almonds, and chocolate. Spoon this mixture into the hollow in the ice cream mold. Cover with wax paper and place the lid tightly on top of the mold, sealing the cracks with softened butter. If you don't have a mold with a lid, use foil or plastic wrap but do remember to seal it very carefully. Bang the mold firmly on the work top to make everything settle evenly. Freeze about 2 hours. To serve, dip the mold in hot water for a few seconds and unmold the cassata onto a platter.

ON THE TERRACE *More than fifty dishes were served – truly characteristic of this extravagant island with its colorful, complex, exuberant cuisine.*

SPUMA GELATA DI PESCHE

Frozen Peach Dessert

SERVES 8

2 envelopes unflavored gelatin
3¼ lb yellow peaches, peeled and pitted
juice of 1 large lemon
¾ cup sugar
3 tablespoons maraschino liqueur
⅔ cup whipping cream, whipped until stiff
sliced peaches, to decorate

Soften the gelatin in a little cold water in a cup according to package directions, then place the cup in a pan of hot water and heat, stirring, until completely dissolved.

Push the peaches through a sieve or vegetable mill to make a smooth purée. Stir in the lemon juice, sugar, and maraschino liqueur. Add the gelatin to the peach mixture and stir well. Fold in the whipped cream carefully.

Pour the mixture into a freezeproof bowl and place in the freezer. Freeze at least 2 hours, removing the dessert every 15 or 20 minutes and stirring it thoroughly.

Transfer into individual ice cream bowls and decorate with sliced peaches to serve.

AFTER THE CEREMONY (above) *Sicilians have a huge capacity for celebrating – and what better occasion could there be than a wedding.*

OUTSIDE THE CHURCH *As the couple leave the church, the guests throw rice at them.*

GELATINA DI MANDORLE

Almond Gelatin

SERVES *8*

*2½ cups blanched almonds
3 cups milk
1¾ cups sugar
2 envelopes unflavored gelatin
3 tablespoons dark rum
1 cup whipping cream whipped until stiff
almond oil for greasing
toasted almonds, to decorate*

Pound the almonds in a mortar until finely crushed, gradually adding a little cold water to prevent the almonds exuding any oil. (If you do this in a food processor be very careful not to allow them to get oily.) Put the almonds in a bowl with the milk and stir together carefully. As soon as the almonds are virtually dissolved into the milk, strain the milk into a bowl through cheesecloth, squeezing the cloth very tightly. (You may need to get somebody to help you do this.)

Add the sugar to the almond milk and stir until it is completely dissolved. Soften the gelatin in a little cold water in a cup according to package directions, then place the cup in a pan of hot water and heat, stirring, until completely dissolved. Whisk the gelatin into the almond mixture and stir well. Stir in the rum, and fold in the whipped cream.

Oil a 1½-quart mold with almond oil, tipping it upside-down to remove any excess. Pour the mixture into the mold and chill 2–3 hours or until set.

Dip the mold into boiling water for a few seconds and unmold onto a platter. (If you don't want to unmold the gelatin, chill it in an unoiled glass bowl.) Decorate with toasted almonds to serve.

GRANITA DI CAFFÈ CON PANNA

Coffee Granita with Whipped Cream

SERVES *8*

*1 cup sugar
2 cups cold water
2½ cups (6 small espresso cups) very strong
espresso coffee
1¼ cups whipping cream
¼ cup confectioners' sugar, sifted
sugar coffee beans, to decorate*

Dissolve the sugar in the water over a low heat. Transfer to a bowl and stir in the coffee. Let cool.

Pour into a shallow metal tray and freeze 2–3 hours. Stir occasionally during this time to prevent the granita becoming too icy. Whip the cream and fold in the confectioners' sugar. Remove the granita from the freezer and spoon into individual dishes. Top with the whipped cream and decorate with sugar coffee beans just before serving.

UN PRANZO A BASE DE PESCE

Seafood Lunch

The southern Italian diet is one of the healthiest in the world. If you set aside for a moment the dreadfully rich desserts, and look at the standard everyday fare, what you come up with is very little meat, lots of vegetables and salads, olive oil instead of butter, and plenty of pasta and fruit. When visiting friends in Palermo recently, I expressed a craving for the incredibly fresh, perfumed fish which seemed to be on offer everywhere. Before I knew it, a wonderful roof-top lunch, with lovely views down to the beach, had been arranged for me. I still can't quite get over how willing Italians are to demonstrate at a moment's notice just how wonderful their food is.

Basking in the warm spring sunshine, we enjoyed the very best that the incredibly blue sea down below had to offer. We began with langoustines, then moved on to the ubiquitous *pasta con le sarde*. This is the most typical of all Sicilian pasta dishes

UP ON THE ROOF (right) *From our table on the roof terrace we could see over to the harbor of Palermo.*

and is made to different recipes on the east and west coasts. As an alternative, there was *vermicelli alla Siracusana*, dressed with all the typical flavors of the south.

A selection of imaginative flavor combinations followed: octopus stewed with mushrooms, a delicately flavored shrimp stew, and fresh baked whiting.

After this wonderful meal, there was only one thing left to do, and that was to wander slowly down to the beach to see how cold the water was, and maybe have an ice cream on the way. . . .

Menu

Scampi Arrosto

Pasta con le Sarde

Vermicelli alla Siracusana

Polpetti in Umido con Funghi

Gamberi in Intingolo

Nasello alla Palermitana

Gelato all'Amarena con il Mango

FISHING BOATS (right) *The seas around Sicily yield many succulent fish, from tiny anchovies to swordfish.*

SCAMPI ARROSTO

Roasted Langoustines

SERVES 6

4½ lb langoustines or jumbo shrimp
4½ cups fresh bread crumbs (white part of the
bread only)

salt and freshly ground pepper
3 tablespoons chopped fresh parsley
4 tablespoons olive oil
grated rind of 1 lemon
lemon wedges, to serve

Ask your fish merchant to prepare the langoustines for you. Wash them thoroughly, then using a very sharp pair of scissors, make an incision down the belly from head to tail.

Mix the bread crumbs with salt, pepper, the parsley, about two-thirds of the oil, and the lemon rind. Fill the incision in each langoustine with this mixture.

Arrange the stuffed langoustines carefully on a wire rack over a roasting pan. Brush them with the rest of the oil and bake in a preheated moderate oven (350°F) about 20 minutes until they are tender.

Serve hot, with wedges of lemon.

PASTA CON LE SARDE

Pasta with Sardines

SERVES 6

1 lb fresh sardines
6–7 large sprigs of fennel
salt
freshly ground pepper
1 large onion, finely chopped
½ cup olive oil
½ teaspoon saffron powder, diluted in a little hot
water
½ cup pine nuts
⅓ cup raisins, soaked in cold water 15 minutes
1 tablespoon anchovy paste
1 lb bucatini or similar pasta, such as uncut
macaroni

Open up and gut the sardines carefully, drawing out the spine and thus removing the head, but keeping them otherwise intact. (Or ask your fish merchant to do this for you.) Rinse and dry them, and set to one side.

Put the fennel in a saucepan with about 2 quarts of water and some salt, bring to a boil, and boil until soft. Remove the fennel from the water, drain, and chop it finely. Keep the water because you will need it to cook the pasta in.

Put the onion into a wide saucepan, cover with cold water, and cook until soft. Add about two-thirds of the olive oil, the saffron, pine nuts, and drained and dried raisins. Stir and cook together about 10 minutes, then add the sardines. Cook about 10 more minutes, turning the sardines over about halfway through, then add the chopped fennel.

Meanwhile, put the anchovy paste and the remaining oil in a separate pan and simmer over a low heat about 5 minutes or until reduced to a runny paste.

Return the pot of fennel-flavored water to the heat and bring to a boil. Toss in the pasta and cook until *al dente* (check package for cooking time as brands vary).

Drain the pasta, put it into a bowl with the sardine sauce and anchovy paste, and toss everything together. Add salt and/or freshly ground pepper to taste. Let rest about 3 minutes before serving.

MENDING NETS *The fishing industry is important to Sicily's economy.*

SCAMPI ARROSTO (far left)

VERMICELLI ALLA SIRACUSANA

Vermicelli with the Sauce of Syracuse

SERVES 6

1 very large yellow sweet pepper or 2 smaller ones
6 tablespoons olive oil
2 cloves garlic, chopped
1 tablespoon anchovy paste
16-oz can tomatoes, drained and cut into small cubes
1 very large eggplant, cut into small cubes
½ cup green olives, coarsely chopped
8 large black olives, coarsely chopped
8 leaves fresh basil, torn to shreds
1 heaped tablespoon capers, rinsed, and chopped
salt
1 lb vermicelli or spaghetti
freshly grated Romano cheese to taste

Hold the pepper on a long-handled fork over a flame, turning it to blister the skin all over. (Alternatively, broil it.) Rub the skin off, then cut the pepper in half and discard seeds and membranes. Cut into thin strips.

Heat the oil in a saucepan over a medium heat and add the garlic, anchovy paste, and the cubed tomatoes and eggplant. Stir and cook 5 or 6 minutes, then add the green and black olives, basil, pepper strips, and capers, and season with salt. Stir and cover. Let simmer 20–25 minutes.

Bring a large pot of salted water to a boil, toss in the pasta, and cook until just *al dente*. Drain. Mix the sauce with the pasta, sprinkle with the Romano cheese, and serve at once.

POLPETTI IN UMIDO CON FUNGHI

Stewed Octopus with Mushrooms

SERVES 6

3 ¼ lb octopus (young and small if
possible)
2 salted anchovies, or 4 anchovy fillets, cleaned and
rinsed thoroughly
1 clove garlic
a small handful of fresh parsley
4 tablespoons red wine
7 tablespoons of olive oil
1 tablespoon tomato paste
salt and freshly ground pepper
2 oz dried funghi porcini, soaked in warm water
15–20 minutes

Clean the octopus, removing the skin, beak, eyes, and sacs. (Or ask your fish merchant to do this for you.) Cut it into even, small sections and rinse it until it becomes completely white. Chop together the anchovies, garlic paste and parsley. Mix with the red wine.

Heat the oil in a heavy-bottomed pan and add the anchovy and garlic mixture. Stir and cook together about 3 minutes, then stir in the tomato paste. Add the octopus sections and season with plenty of salt and pepper. Cover and simmer about 45 minutes. Check occasionally and add more water if the stew appears to be drying out.

Drain the *funghi porcini* and rinse them thoroughly. Add them to the stew, cover the pan again, and cook a further 20 minutes. Serve hot.

GAMBERI IN INTINGOLO

Stewed Shrimp

SERVES 4–6

2 tablespoons butter
1 tablespoon olive oil
1 onion, chopped
1 carrot, chopped
4 sprigs of fresh parsley, chopped
2¼ lb large shrimp, peeled (heads on)
salt and freshly ground pepper
⅔ cup dry white wine
2 tablespoons tomato paste
1 tablespoon all-purpose flour
4 slices of white bread, crusts removed
vegetable oil for frying

Heat half the butter and all the olive oil in a skillet and fry the onion, carrot, and parsley until soft. Add the shrimp and stir together carefully. Season with salt and pepper and add the wine. As soon as the wine has evaporated remove from the heat.

Take the heads off all the shrimp and set the shrimp aside. Put the heads in a food processor or mortar. Add the tomato paste and a few tablespoons of hot water and press or pound the heads to make a smooth purée. Pour this purée into a saucepan and add the vegetable mixture. Knead the remaining butter to a paste with the flour and add to the pan. Bring to a boil, stirring constantly, until thickened. Add the shrimp and stir to heat through.

Cut the bread into small triangles and fry in the hot oil until crisp.

Arrange the shrimp in the center of a dish and garnish with the bread around the edge. Serve at once.

NASELLO ALLA PALERMITANA

Whiting Cooked in the Style of Palermo

*This dish can also be prepared with small mackerel
or silver hake.*

SERVES 6

1 large whiting or individual whitings, weighing
about 2 ¾ lb in total, drawn
olive oil
fresh rosemary
salt and freshly ground pepper
5 teaspoons anchovy paste, or 5 salted or canned
anchovies, rinsed and cleaned
¼ cup dried bread crumbs

Rub the inside of the fish carefully with oil. Insert a small branch of rosemary inside each fish and sprinkle the inside of the fish with salt and pepper. Oil an ovenproof dish and lay the fish in it.

Put about 4 tablespoons of oil in a small saucepan and add the anchovy paste or cleaned anchovies. Cook and mash this mixture with a fork to reduce to a smooth purée. Pour this over and inside the fish. Sprinkle with the bread crumbs and a few leaves of rosemary and a little more salt and pepper.

Place the dish in a preheated moderate oven (325°F) and bake about 30 minutes. Serve hot.

GELATO ALL'AMARENA CON IL MANGO

GELATO ALL'AMARENA CON IL MANGO

Mangoes with Cherry Ice Cream

SERVES 6

Ice Cream
1 lb (2 pints) very ripe fresh cherries
2 cups whipping cream
4 –5 tablespoons sugar
1 cup confectioners' sugar

6 small mangoes

To make the ice cream, pit the cherries and reduce them to a purée in a blender or food processor. Whip the cream with the sugar until it is stiff.

Fold the cream into the cherry purée and add the confectioners' sugar very gradually, folding it in carefully. Transfer to a shallow metal tray and freeze about 2 hours, taking it out and whisking it energetically every 30 minutes.

Next prepare the mangoes. With a very sharp knife, make 8 cuts through the skin and flesh of each mango, working lengthwise from top to bottom but not cutting right through at the end with the stalk attached. Then pull back each segment to achieve the effect of an open flower. Cut out the seed, removing with it as little flesh as possible.

Place each mango on a plate. Cut the flesh away from each "petal", by sliding a knife between the skin and the fruit three-quarters of the way down. Chill until required. To serve, fill the center of each "flower" with ice cream.

UNA FESTA TRA AMICI

Just a Party

In a huge, ancient garden in Tuscany, filled with thin, crooked pine trees, stands a blue-shuttered house – La Dogana Estense. This used to be my grandparents' house when my grandfather was in government, and during the summer it was always used to entertain their many friends. Sadly, I never knew my grandparents, but my uncle inherited the villa and continued the tradition of using it as a summer house to which all his friends and acquaintances would be invited.

Apart from the delicious food which was always prepared for these occasions, my most lasting impression of those parties was of their relaxed, casual air. I remember such good conversations and guests who were content simply to enjoy the house, the company, the wonderful food and wine. The villa seemed to assume the role of a miniature gastronomic center with incredible ease, and the atmosphere of unruffled elegance and pleasure has seeped into the walls themselves. It is to this day the best place to have a party, and I was delighted to be able to borrow it for one of my own gatherings.

I knew I had to devise a menu that was worthy of the loveliness

LA DOGANA ESTENSE (left)
Wonderful food and good conversation are what I have always associated with my grandparents' house.

of the setting, so I decided to recreate some of the dishes I remember enjoying here on other occasions when I was not the hostess. I arranged all the dishes as a buffet and allowed everybody to

help themselves, beginning with the antipasti and first courses. I then served a tender roast of veal threaded through with pistachio nuts and as an alternative for vegetarians, or accompanying

vegetables for meat eaters, there was a layered dish of zucchini with mozzarella, tomato, and basil. The huge tomato salad was dressed in pesto sauce and had pine nuts scattered over it for added crunch.

After a pause I served my two desserts: a light and cooling raspberry bavarois and the most authentic *zuppa inglese* I could muster. The conversation flowed all around me, the wine seemed to match the dishes to perfection – I retired, certain that my grandparents would have been proud of me.

Menu

Insalata di Mozzarella, Olive e Rucola

Gamberi con i Fagioli

Penne al Gorgonzola

Corona di Riso con il Granchio

Pomodori in Insalata con il Pesto e i Pinoli

Arrosto di Vitello con Pistacchi

Parmigiana di Zucchine

Bavarese al Lampone

La Zuppa Inglese

BAVARESE AL LAMPONE (left)

INSALATA DI MOZZARELLA, OLIVE E RUCOLA

Mozzarella Salad with Black Olives and Arugula

SERVES 6

1 lb mozzarella cheese, well drained
⅔ cup large black olives, pitted
2 large handfuls of arugula, trimmed, washed, and torn into pieces
9 tablespoons olive oil
salt and freshly ground pepper

Cut the mozzarella into cubes about the size of a cherry. Mix with the olives and arugula leaves in a bowl. Pour over the olive oil and season with salt and pepper. Toss everything together carefully, using 2 spoons. Let stand about 1 hour, and toss together once more just before serving.

CRATES OF FRESHLY PICKED OLIVES (left) *In Tuscany olives are generally hand-picked by workers standing on tall ladders.*

MARBLE KITCHEN (right) *A pot of parsley is left to drain in the marble sink of the villa's cool and elegant kitchen.*

GAMBERI CON I FAGIOLI

Shrimp with White Beans

SERVES 6

*1½ cups dried navy beans, soaked overnight in cold
water, or canned cannellini beans
2¼ lb medium shrimp
salt and freshly ground pepper
1 tablespoon white wine vinegar
1 clove garlic, very finely chopped
2 tablespoons chopped fresh parsley
5 tablespoons olive oil
juice of ½ lemon*

Drain the soaked beans, rinse them thoroughly in cold water, and put them in a saucepan. Cover with fresh cold water. Bring to a boil and boil very fast 5 or 6 minutes, then drain and rinse them again. Return them to the saucepan, cover with fresh water, and return to a boil. Simmer until tender but not mushy – this takes about 30–40 minutes. (If you are using canned beans, just drain and rinse them gently before using.)

Meanwhile, put the shrimp into a pan of cold water with a pinch of salt and the vinegar. Bring to a boil and cook until a white foam appears on the surface. Drain them and peel them at once, while they are still hot. Put them to one side.

Drain the cooked beans and put them into a bowl. Add the shrimp, the garlic, parsley, oil, lemon juice, and salt and pepper to taste. Toss everything together and let stand about 1 hour. Toss everything together once more just before serving.

PENNE AL GORGONZOLA

Pasta Quills with Gorgonzola

SERVES 6

*½ lb (1 cup) ricotta cheese
5 oz gorgonzola cheese
4 tablespoons milk
1 small onion, very finely chopped
1 stalk celery, very finely chopped
salt and freshly ground pepper
1 lb pasta quills (penne)*

Put the ricotta and the gorgonzola into a food processor or blender with the milk, onion, celery, and salt and pepper to taste. Process until quite smooth.

Bring a large pot of salted water to a rolling boil. Toss in the pasta, stir to prevent sticking, and boil until *al dente* (check package for timing as different brands vary.)

Drain the pasta and dress it with the gorgonzola sauce. Toss everything together very thoroughly and serve at once.

CORONA DI RISO CON IL GRANCHIO

Crown of Rice with Crab

SERVES 6

*4 tablespoons olive oil
2 cloves garlic
½ dried small chili pepper
2½ cups puréed tomatoes
salt
3 cups brown or white long-grain rice
3 tablespoons butter
1¾ lb cooked crab meat, fresh or frozen*

Heat the oil, garlic, and chili pepper together in a saucepan about 5 minutes. Add the puréed tomatoes, stir, and partly cover. Simmer about 15–20 minutes or until reduced.

Meanwhile, bring a large pot of salted water to a boil. Toss in the rice and cook until tender but not mushy. Drain very carefully and return to the saucepan. Add the butter and toss together. Spoon the rice into a 1½-quart metal ring mold, press it down firmly, and let it stand about 4 minutes.

Remove the chili pepper from the sauce. Add the crab to the tomato sauce and heat through about 5 minutes. Unmold the ring of rice onto a large platter, pour the crab and tomato sauce all over the rice crown, and serve at once.

CORONA DI RISO CON IL GRANCHIO (left)

POMODORI IN INSALATA CON IL PESTO E I PINOLI

Tomato Salad with Pesto and Pine Nuts

SERVES *6*

4 large Marmande or other flavorful tomatoes
2 tablespoons pesto sauce
5 tablespoons olive oil
freshly ground black pepper
2 tablespoons pine nuts
a few fresh basil leaves

Cut the tomatoes into equal slices. Put the sliced tomatoes in a bowl. Mix the pesto and olive oil together and pour it all over the tomatoes. Toss everything together thoroughly. Add ground black pepper to taste and toss again.

Scatter the pine nuts and fresh basil leaves over the salad and then let it stand until required. Toss the salad again just before serving.

GAMBERI CON I FAGIOLI (above), PARMIGIANA DI ZUCCHINE (below left), ARROSTO DI VITELLO CON PISTACCHI (below right)

ARROSTO DI VITELLO CON PISTACCHI

Pot Roast Veal with Pistachio Nuts

SERVES *6*

2 lb boneless veal roast
2 oz pork fatback, cut into long strips
3 tablespoons shelled, unsalted pistachio nuts
3 sprigs of fresh rosemary
salt and freshly ground pepper
3 tablespoons butter
2 tablespoons olive oil
1 carrot, finely chopped
1 onion, finely chopped
a mixture of fresh or dried herbs: bay leaf, rosemary and sage (if fresh, tie them together with thread so as to be able to remove them easily)
¼ cup brandy
1¼ cups meat or vegetable stock

Pierce the meat all over with a sharp-pointed knife and insert strips of pork fatback, pistachios, and rosemary alternately into each hole. When the meat is generously threaded through, season it generously, and tie it into shape securely with cook's thread.

Heat the butter and oil in a flameproof casserole and add the vegetables and herbs. Fry until the vegetables are soft, then add the veal roast and seal it all over. Add the brandy and cook 2–3 minutes until the fumes have evaporated, then add the stock. Cover and simmer about 20 minutes. Turn the meat over and cook a further 20 minutes.

Let the meat cool in the casserole, then slice it thinly. Arrange on a platter and serve.

PARMIGIANA DI ZUCCHINE

Zucchini with Tomato, Mozzarella, and Parmesan

SERVES 6

6 large zucchini, sliced
1¼ cups cooking oil for frying
4 tablespoons olive oil
2 cloves garlic, minced
2½ cups puréed tomatoes
a handful of fresh basil leaves
a large pinch of dried oregano
salt and freshly milled pepper
1 lb mozzarella cheese, drained and thinly sliced
about 1¼ cups freshly grated Parmesan cheese

Heat the frying oil until sizzling, then fry the zucchini until golden brown – about 3 minutes each side. Drain and reserve.

Heat the olive oil and garlic together in a saucepan about 4 minutes without browning the garlic, then add the puréed tomatoes and stir. Add half the basil and the oregano. Season to taste and partly cover. Simmer until reduced and no longer watery – about 10 minutes.

Put a thin layer of the tomato sauce in the bottom of a shallow ovenproof dish. Arrange some slices of fried zucchini on top and cover with mozzarella slices, then with a little more tomato sauce. Add a few basil leaves and finish with a generous coating of Parmesan cheese. Repeat until all the ingredients are used up, finishing with a layer of tomato and basil.

Bake in a preheated moderate oven (350°F) 20–30 minutes or until the mozzarella is melted and stringy. Serve immediately.

BAVARESE AL LAMPONE

Raspberry Bavarois

SERVES 6

1 lb (2 pints) fresh or frozen raspberries
grated rind and juice of ½ orange
1¾ cups confectioners' sugar, sifted
2 envelopes unflavored gelatin
1¼ cups whipping cream
3 tablespoons sugar
olive or almond oil for greasing
raspberries and orange slices for decoration

Push the raspberries through a nylon sieve into a bowl and mix the purée with the orange rind and juice, and the sifted confectioners' sugar. Set aside.

Soften the gelatin in a little cold water in a cup according to package directions, then place the cup in a pan of hot water and heat, stirring, until the gelatin is completely dissolved. Add the gelatin to the berry mixture and stir it all together very thoroughly. Place the bowl in a cool place or on some ice to help it set quickly.

Meanwhile, whip the cream and add the sugar. As soon as the berry mixture has begun to set, fold the cream into it with care.

Grease a 1½ quart mold very lightly with oil and spoon the mixture into the mold. Bang the mold down on the work top to settle the contents evenly. Cover and put it in the refrigerator at least 4 hours.

Dip the mold into boiling water 5 seconds to loosen it, then unmold the bavarois onto a platter. Decorate with raspberries and orange slices.

LA ZUPPA INGLESE

Italian Trifle

SERVES 6

3 eggs, separated
1¼ cups sugar
6 tablespoons all-purpose flour, sifted
2 cups milk
7 oz sponge cake, cut into fingers ¼ inch thick
2 tablespoons rum
2 tablespoons of a liqueur of your choice
¼ cup chopped mixed candied peel

Beat the egg yolks with ½ cup of the sugar, the flour, and ½ cup of the milk until smooth. Heat the rest of the milk until just boiling, then stir it into the egg yolk mixture. Return to the heat in the top of a double boiler and cook, stirring constantly, until the custard is thick enough to coat the spoon. Set aside to cool. Beat the egg whites until stiff, then fold in the remaining sugar. Chill until required.

Lay half of the cake fingers in one plate and the other half in another. Pour the rum over one plate and the liqueur over the other.

In a 12–inch ovenproof dish, spread a layer of custard, then a layer of cake, a further layer of custard, a sprinkling of candied fruit and so on, until only the beaten egg white is left. Pile this on top of the layered trifle. Bake in a preheated very cool oven (275°F) about 20 minutes or until golden and crisp. Serve cold.

LADEN BUFFET TABLE *I wanted this party to have a relaxed atmosphere and so let everyone help themselves to the various courses.*

IL COMPLEANNO VENEZIANO DI MARIA

Maria's Venetian Birthday

My friend Maria comes from Venice, and on her birthday we asked another friend who is a professional cook to create for her the ultimate Venetian menu. The results were nothing short of spectacular.

Venetian cooking has two different facets – a simple, homey side in which uncomplicated, filling dishes of vegetables, beans, and rice predominate, and a totally contrasting, complex cuisine with more than a hint of ancient splendor and exotic spices from the foreign lands whose ships were once frequent visitors to its port.

The Veneto's most famous dish is, of course, risotto, with countless different combinations of ingredients. I was taught how to make risotto at an early age by a friend of the family who comes from the Veneto area. At the tender age of seven I used to stand on a stool at his elbow and watch him stir and stir, tipping in ladlefuls of stock just at the moment when he told me to do so, and not a second before. As we worked he would tell me the rules: how the rice must be allowed to stick to the bottom a little, how the

surface must ripple like waves, how to let the rice fluff up once it has finished cooking.

For Maria's birthday dinner we dined off antique white lace in a setting which was suitably evocative of a Venetian palazzo, a theme which was taken up in the Doges' soup which began the meal. The amazing purple-red color of this soup comes from beets, which is a fairly unusual ingredient in Italy anyway, but the addition of other vegetables and balls of fried rice make it really very different indeed.

Monkfish is widely used in the Venice area and a stunning dish of monkfish flavored with fresh mint followed the soup. Another herb, sage, was used in the simple chicken dish which was our main course, accompanied by the ubiquitous Venetian sweet and sour pearl onions.

As a birthday cake, Maria wanted a classic Venetian cake

POTS AND PANS (left) *Gleaming pots and pans, the legacy of a previous generation of cooks, hang ready for use on the kitchen wall.*

118

called *fugazza di fichi*. *Fugazza* is the Venetian word for focaccia, which can mean cake as well as flat pizza bread. There are all kinds of *fugazzas* made in the Veneto area, the most traditional being the *fugazza della Befana*. This very plain cake is traditionally made for Twelfth Night, or January 6. During this night the old woman Befana is supposed to come down the chimney, bringing presents for all the good children – and sacks of coal for those who have been naughty. So that she finds the cake ready to eat when she comes, the *fugazza* is traditionally wrapped in cabbage leaves then put in the embers of the fire to cook. Maria could remember how the Befana's arrival was prepared for in this way when she was a child, and the *fugazza di fichi* reminded her very much of her Venetian childhood.

Menu

Zuppa dei Dogi

Coda di Rospo alla Menta

Cipolline Agrodolce

Pollo alla Salvia

Fugazza di Fichi

DINING ROOM *Our dinner for Maria had a setting evocative of the splendor of a Venetian palazzo.*

ZUPPA DEI DOGI

Doges' Soup

SERVES 6

¾ cup long-grain white rice
½ cup grated fontina or Edam cheese
½ egg
¼ cup freshly grated Parmesan cheese
1 tablespoon olive oil
1½ quarts clear meat broth
1 large beet, boiled, peeled, and cut into matchsticks
2 carrots, cut into matchsticks
1 large leek, cut into matchsticks
¼ lb celeriac (celery root), peeled and cut into matchsticks
4–6 tablespoons all-purpose flour
oil for deep frying

Cook the rice in boiling water about 10 minutes or until still fairly firm in the middle; drain. Mix the rice with the fontina until very well blended, then add the egg, Parmesan, and olive oil. Mix very thoroughly. Shape the mixture into walnut-sized balls – you may find you have to squeeze it in your hands so that it sticks together. Chill the balls in the refrigerator until required.

To make the soup, bring the broth to a boil in a large pot, add the vegetable matchsticks, and simmer 10 minutes.

Meanwhile, remove the rice balls from the refrigerator and coat them with flour. (Be sure to handle them carefully so that they do not break up.)

Deep fry in very hot oil until golden. Drain on paper towels. Place the rice balls in soup plates and ladle the soup over them. Serve immediately.

PREPARING THE MEAL (left) *The Venetian menu which Alessandro devised was inspired by old and new sources.*

RICE BALLS (below) *Rice dishes, especially superb risottos, figure prominently in Venetian cuisine, and in this soup the deep-fried rice balls add a rich and individual note.*

ZUPPA DEI DOGI (right)

CODA DI ROSPO ALLA MENTA

Minted Monkfish

SERVES 6

3 lb cleaned boneless monkfish
3 tablespoons olive oil
about 10 leaves fresh mint
1 cup white wine
1 teaspoon saffron powder, or a large pinch of
saffron threads steeped in 2 tablespoons hot water
1 cup whipping cream
salt

Beginning from the tail end, cut the fish into angular wedges. Heat the olive oil in a skillet with half the mint leaves. Add the monkfish and fry it quickly to seal all sides, turning it over several times to prevent sticking. Add the wine and saffron powder or liquid and simmer about 15–20 minutes or until the monkfish is tender.

Remove the fish from the pan and keep it warm. Add the cream to the pan and simmer to reduce the sauce by about half. Add salt to taste.

Arrange the fish on a warm serving dish and place a fresh leaf of mint between each slice. Discard the mint leaves from the sauce and pour it around the fish. Serve at once.

SHUTTERED APARTMENT (left) *Even in elegant squares the washing still has to be dried.*

After adding the wine and saffron liquid to the monkfish, simmer about 15–20 minutes.

CODA DI ROSPO ALLA MENTA (below)

CIPOLLINE AGRODOLCE

Sweet and Sour Onions

SERVES 6

24 very large scallions or pearl onions
¼ cup sugar
⅓ cup white wine vinegar
1⅓ cups water
6–8 cloves
2 bay leaves
10–12 juniper berries
a pinch of salt

Wash and trim the onions, removing the green part. Cut the bulbs in half. Put all the other ingredients in a saucepan and boil 1 minute, then add the onions. Cover and simmer 10–12 minutes. Serve hot.

POLLO ALLA SALVIA

Sage Chicken

SERVES *6*

1 young chicken, weighing about 2¼ lb, cut up
1 tablespoon cooking oil
1½ tablespoons butter, softened
1 cup dry white wine
2 oz prosciutto crudo, sliced into thin strips
6–8 fresh sage leaves
salt and freshly ground pepper

Rinse and dry the chicken pieces carefully. Heat the oil and butter in a skillet and brown the chicken pieces all over very thoroughly. Drain off most of the fat and add the wine to the pan. Then add the prosciutto crudo and the sage leaves. Season to taste.

Cover and simmer gently until the chicken is cooked through, about 30–40 minutes. Serve at once.

POLLO ALLA SALVIA, *served with green salad.*

FUGAZZA DI FICHI

Venetian Fig Cake

SERVES 8–10

3 eggs
1¼ cups milk
¾ cup sugar
6 tablespoons Grand Marnier
5 tablespoons butter, softened
2¾ cups all-purpose flour

2 heaped teaspoons baking powder
½ lb dried figs, soaked in warm water 10 minutes
⅔ cup raisins, soaked in warm water 10 minutes
butter for greasing
flour for dusting
confectioners' sugar for coating

Remove the cake from the pan to cool (below left).

FUGAZZA DI FICHI (below)

Beat the eggs until completely blended. Add the milk, sugar, and Grand Marnier and mix thoroughly. Then add the soft butter and beat well. Gradually mix in the flour and baking powder. Stir in the drained dried fruit and mix together thoroughly.

Butter a 12–inch cake pan and dust with flour. Pour in the cake batter and smooth the surface. Bake in a preheated moderate oven (350°F) 40–60 minutes.

Remove the cake from the pan and cool completely on a wire rack. Coat with sifted confectioners' sugar to serve.

IL PRANZO DOMENICALE
IN GIARDINO

Sunday Lunch in the Garden

Every time I go home to Ronchi, in Tuscany, I try to invite my local friends over to catch up on their news and let them know what's happening in my own life. There really is nothing better on a sunny spring day than to sit out under the trees in the garden and eat delicious, simply cooked food with a group of old friends who have a lot of catching up to do.

It is no secret to anyone who knows me just how strongly I feel about this house where I spent much of my childhood. It was here that my passion for good food and wine began. Growing up here meant being involved in a constant bustle around the kitchen, because there never seemed to be fewer than about fifteen people for any meal. As a very small and curious three-year-old, I would peer around the door to see what was happening. Far from being shooed away, I would be greeted gladly and immediately given a job to do – peeling potatoes, shelling peas, or scraping barnacles off piles of shiny black mussels. Whatever it was, I was just thrilled to be a part of the whirl of activity.

When it came to the actual meal, I would sit proudly at my end of the table and wait impatiently for the moment when the food would be brought in. I can remember so clearly the warm feeling of immense pride which would wash right over me, knowing that I had had a part in the preparation, however small. I still get the same feeling every time I place a finished dish on the table for family or friends.

On this late spring day we were right in the middle of the strawberry season, so I decided to make a strawberry risotto as a first course. This may sound odd, but in fact risottos made with fruit are quite common and widely appreciated all over Italy these days. The addition of plenty of robust red wine brings out the flavor of the fruit even more acutely. I like it with lots of freshly grated Parmesan sprinkled over the top, but this addition is entirely optional as it is a matter of personal taste.

An early morning trip to the fish market yielded some wonderful *orata*, one of my favorite fish, which in spite of its name of gilt-head bream is actually covered in silvery scales. (Red snapper is an alternative for the recipe given here if you cannot find *orata*.) The fish was stuffed with fennel and garlic, seasoned, then moistened with olive oil and white wine. Wrapped in foil, it was then baked until tender. From the vegetable garden I picked a huge basketful of lettuce and lots of fresh basil, along with arugula, which I love for the distinctive flavor it adds to salads. The dressing was lemon juice and olive oil. This salad and a dish of crispy roast potatoes with lemon and rosemary were the perfect partners for the fish.

One of my favorite combinations is hot and cold foods eaten together, and the dessert bore out my theory on how delicious this can be. I made a very lemony soufflé and served it piping hot with a dish of fresh, tangy lemon sorbet. The only complaint to be heard from my guests was that I did not make enough.

Menu

Risotto di Fragole

Orata al Forno con il Finocchio

Patate Arrosto al Limone e Rosmarino

Insalata Verde

Soffiato al Limone

Granita al Limone

LUNCH AL FRESCO (left) *Sunday is the perfect day for a leisurely lunch in the garden to catch up on gossip with old friends.*

FRESH STRAWBERRIES (left) *lend themselves beautifully to a wide variety of dishes, the more unusual strawberry risotto among them.*

RISOTTO DI FRAGOLE

Strawberry Risotto

SERVES 6

4 tablespoons unsalted butter
1 small onion, or 2 shallots, finely chopped
2 cups risotto (arborio) rice
1 lb (3½–4 cups) strawberries, hulled
1¾ cups red wine
1 quart hot chicken or vegetable stock
⅓ cup whipping cream
6 tablespoons freshly grated Parmesan cheese
salt and freshly ground black pepper

Melt the butter in a heavy-bottomed saucepan and fry the onion or shallots until soft and translucent. Add the rice and stir to coat it with butter and onion. Slice half the strawberries thinly and stir them into the rice, then add half the wine. Cook until the strawberries become pulpy and the wine is absorbed.

Add the remaining wine and stir to mix. When the wine has been absorbed by the rice, begin to add the hot stock, ladle by ladle. Stir each ladleful of stock into the rice, let it become absorbed, and then add more stock. Don't rush this process.

When all the stock has been added and the rice is about 3 minutes from being ready, stir in almost all the remaining strawberries and let them become soft and pulpy. Stir in the cream and Parmesan. Add a little salt and plenty of freshly ground black pepper.

Arrange the risotto on a platter, garnish with the reserved strawberries, and serve at once, with extra Parmesan if desired.

ORATA AL FORNO CON IL FINOCCHIO

Baked Sea Bream with Fennel

SERVES 6

*2 gilt-head bream or red snapper, weighing about
3¼ lb in total, drawn
6 tablespoons olive oil
2 large bulbs of fennel, very thinly sliced
⅓ cup dry white wine
salt and freshly ground pepper
4 cloves garlic, sliced in half*

Wash the fish carefully and pat dry. Line an ovenproof dish with foil, leaving enough overlapping to wrap and cover the fish completely but very loosely. Oil the foil lightly on the inside and then lay the fish on top. Stuff the fish with fennel slices, and arrange the remaining fennel under and around the fish. Pour the wine all around the fish. Oil the inside and outside of the fish thoroughly. Sprinkle with salt and pepper, inside and out. Put some of the garlic inside the fish and place the rest around the fish.

Close the foil over the fish and bake in a preheated moderate oven (350°F) about 1 hour or until the fish is cooked through. Serve hot, unwrapping at the table for the best effect.

RISOTTO DI FRAGOLE (left)

ORATA *It was worth going to the market early for the superbly fresh fish which were on offer.*

ORATA AL FORNO CON IL FINOCCHIO *Cooking the fish in foil keeps in all the delicious flavors. When you open the parcel at the table, the aniseed aroma of fennel is released.*

PATATE ARROSTO AL LIMONE E ROSMARINO

Roast Potatoes with Lemon and Rosemary

SERVES 6

*12 medium-sized potatoes, peeled
½ cup olive oil
2 lemons, thickly sliced
a large spring of rosemary, broken into small sections
salt
freshly ground pepper*

Cut the potatoes in half lengthwise and then in half again so as to make segment shapes. Put them into a bowl and pour the oil over them; roll them in the oil with your hands to coat them very thoroughly. Tip the potatoes into a roasting pan and add the lemon slices, putting them underneath the potato segments as much as possible. Put the rosemary sections here and there and season the potatoes generously with salt and pepper.

Place the pan in a preheated hot oven (425°F) and bake about 50-60 minutes, turning the potatoes over occasionally. When cooked they will be lightly browned and tender all the way through.

INSALATA VERDE

Special Green Salad

SERVES 6

4 hearts of crisp lettuce
a handful of fresh basil leaves
a handful of arugula leaves
8 scallions, green parts only
2 tablespoons white wine vinegar
½ teaspoon salt
3 cloves garlic, crushed with the side of a knife
½ teaspoon coarse-grain mustard
6–8 tablespoons olive oil
freshly ground black pepper

Shred the lettuce very thinly with a sharp knife. Arrange it on a wide, flattish platter. Tear the basil into pieces and scatter it on the top. Chop the arugula coarsely and scatter it on the lettuce. Slice the green part of the scallions into small sections and sprinkle this all over the top. Cover the salad and place in the refrigerator until required.

Mix the wine vinegar and salt together until the salt has dissolved, then add the crushed garlic and stir. Add the mustard and stir again, then continue to stir as you pour in the oil. Add freshly ground pepper to taste and let the dressing stand about 30 minutes before removing the garlic.

Pour the dressing over the salad and toss well. Serve immediately.

SOFFIATO AL LIMONE

Lemon Soufflé

SERVES 6

2 tablespoons butter
2 tablespoons all-purpose flour
1¼ cups milk
grated rind and juice of 2 lemons
6 tablespoons sugar
3 egg yolks
4 egg whites
butter for greasing

Melt the butter in a heavy-bottomed pan until foaming. Add the flour and stir until smooth, then add the milk and cook, stirring constantly, until thick. Remove from the heat and mix in the lemon rind and juice and sugar very thoroughly. Stir in the egg yolks one at a time. Beat the egg whites until stiff and fold gently into the lemon mixture.

Butter a six-portion soufflé dish very thoroughly, then pour in the lemon mixture. Bake in the center of a preheated moderately hot oven (375°F) about 35-40 minutes or until golden and well risen. Serve immediately, alongside the ice-cold sorbet.

SUNDAY LUNCH IN THE GARDEN

GRANITA AL LIMONE

Lemon Sorbet

SERVES *6*

1¼ cups sugar
2½ cups water
grated rind of 1 lemon
juice of 2 lemons

Heat the sugar and water together over a very low heat, stirring, until the sugar has completely dissolved. Then boil gently 10 minutes until a light syrup has formed. Pour the syrup into a bowl and let it cool completely.

Stir the lemon rind and juice into the syrup. Pour into ice-cube trays (with dividers removed) or other shallow metal trays. Leave about 40 minutes, until it is half-frozen, then remove and stir thoroughly. Return to the freezer for 2 hours before serving.

SALAD FROM THE GARDEN (opposite left) *The delicious salad of lettuce, basil, and arugula leaves was eaten not far from the spot where they had been picked.*

MARKET ON WHEELS (right) *These little pick-ups travel around towns with a loudspeaker to advertise their wares.*

131

LA FESTA DELLA VIGILIA DI NATALE

Christmas Eve Feast

There is a proverb in Italy which says, "Spend Christmas with your family and Easter with whoever you want." It underlines the feeling that Christmas is above everything else a time of togetherness, the most important family gathering of the year.

The main Christmas celebration in Italy is on Christmas Eve rather than Christmas Day, and revolves around midnight mass. A great sense of importance is attached to this mass, which is debatedly the second most important in the Catholic calendar. It has social as well as religious importance, however, as this is an occasion for dressing up and being seen – whole families set off for church together in their finery. It is not until they return after midnight that the real Christmas feast begins, with presents exchanged and opened over a long luxurious dinner.

Preparation obviously begins early in the day and the excitement gradually builds up as everyone joins in and the kitchen really starts to bubble with activity. Each member of the family who arrives brings something to add to the already groaning side-

CRIB *At Christmas time many children set up a nativity scene which then decorates the house over the festive period.*

board – someone may turn up with a very special *panettone*, or in our family someone may have detoured via Siena to collect some amazing cookies and pastries. Presents are already piled under the Christmas tree, closely watched by the children for whom the food that is to come is much less of a concern than the colorfully wrapped gifts. When everything is finally ready, it's time to set the table with the very best tablecloth and china.

Christmas is first and foremost a time for the children, so an attempt is made to give them their supper at around seven o'clock in the evening – although this rarely means that they go to bed and sleep. Some families are very strict and do not allow the children to unwrap a single present until they return from mass. In other families, parents relent and let the little ones open a parcel or two before the adults set off for church. When they eventually return home, it is usually to find the children wide awake and raring to go – this is their present-opening moment!

As you can imagine, the adults may be feeling fairly tired by the time the excited children have at last been packed off to bed. They invariably revive, however, at the thought of the feast to come. The traditional foods for Christmas Eve dinner vary enormously from one area of Italy to the next. As it

is a religious occasion, many families still do not eat meat, but base their meal on fish, with delicious salads and vegetable dishes to accompany it, and all over the country one finds countless local specialties. In Rome, for instance, *capitone*, a giant eel, is served in a marinade of vinegar, bay leaves, and garlic; in Calabria, I once had a wonderful Christmas salad called a *mappina*. The sight of shop windows filling up with beautifully decorated boxes of various cakes, chocolates and cookies is a sure sign that Christmas is approaching, and while many of them are Sienese in origin, there will be infinite local specialities, too.

In recent years, however, the northern European and American tradition of serving poultry at Christmas has gradually been adopted by families throughout Italy, including mine. We certainly kept to tradition as far as our antipasti were concerned, with marinated herrings and paper-thin slices of raw, marinated swordfish to start the meal. To follow, there were freshly made *tortellini in brodo*, pasta hats in a chicken broth, and my aching arms bore witness to the effort I had put into making huge quantities of *tortellini* that afternoon. The alternative was *linguine* with red and black caviar, which looked every bit as good as it tasted. The Veneto area is noted

for its excellent poultry dishes and for our main course we had the wonderfully festive *faraona alla Veronese*, guinea fowl with colorful green peppers.

Italians love desserts and as Christmas is one of *the* times of the year for indulging, the dessert had to be something very special. And it was – literally a mountain of feathery light chestnut purée and whipped cream, with a dusting of chocolate. And of course at Christmas you just have to have a sliver of the deliciously rich *panforte*, or perhaps a slice of light *panettone*. And there is always *pandoro* – a Veronese cake similar to *panettone* – to set off arguments about their relative merits. Everyone eventually mellows, however, over a concluding glass or two of amber-colored *vin santo*, with perhaps just a little almond-studded Cantucci biscuit to dip in and help it on its way.

Menu

Aringhe Marinate

Carpaccio di Pesce Spada

Linguine al Caviale Rosso e Nero or *Tortellini in Brodo*

Spinaci alla Genovese

Cipolle Arrosto

Faraona alla Veronese

Il Montebianco

Panforte

ARINGHE MARINATE

Marinated Herrings

SERVES 6

12 small (or 6 medium-sized) fresh herrings, dressed
butter for greasing
1 onion, thinly sliced
2 lemons, thinly sliced
Marinade
2 tablespoons butter
¼ lb carrots, peeled and sliced into rounds
a pinch of dried thyme
a pinch of cayenne
1 bay leaf
1 tablespoon all-purpose flour
2 cups dry white wine
3 tablespoons wine vinegar
1 tablespoon salt
1 teaspoon sugar
1 shallot, finely chopped
2 tablespoons chopped fresh parsley
1 teaspoon chopped fresh cilantro
a pinch of ground cinnamon
4 cloves
a pinch of dried marjoram

Melt the butter in a pan, add the carrots, thyme, cayenne, and bay leaf, and fry until the carrots are softened but not colored. Sprinkle with the flour and stir to brown it lightly, then pour on the wine and the vinegar, stirring well. Bring to a boil and boil 2 minutes.

Add the salt, sugar, shallot, parsley, cilantro, cinnamon, and cloves and stir to mix everything together. Simmer the marinade very gently about 40 minutes to reduce the volume of liquid by about one-third.

FISH STALL *Traditionally fish features prominently in the Christmas Eve menu.*

Wash and dry the herrings carefully and arrange them in a flameproof dish or pan in a single layer. Stir the marjoram into the boiling hot marinade and pour it over the fish. Cover with a sheet of buttered parchment paper. Place the dish on a very low heat and simmer 12 minutes. Remove from the heat and cool completely.

Arrange the fish carefully on a platter and cover with the strained marinade. Chill at least 24 hours before serving.

Garnish with the sliced onion and lemons, and serve with plenty of crusty bread.

CARPACCIO DI PESCE SPADA

Swordfish Carpaccio

Order the slices of swordfish in advance from your fish merchant.

SERVES 6

12 wafer-thin slices of fresh swordfish
juice of 1 lime
juice of ½ large lemon
salt and freshly ground pepper
1 cup olive oil
3 tablespoons chopped fresh parsley

Arrange the fish in a layer in a platter deep enough to take the oil and juice as well as the fish. Allow the slices to overlap slightly. Mix the lime and lemon juices together and add about ½ teaspoon of salt, though you may prefer to add more or leave it out altogether. Stir until the juice has completely dissolved the salt. Pour this all over the fish in as even a stream as possible. Turn each slice over to make sure it is covered completely. Grind plenty of black pepper on top, then cover the fish with a layer of olive oil.

Leave the fish slices to marinate a minimum of 2 hours, preferably not in the refrigerator. If you do refrigerate the dish, make sure to bring it back to room temperature before serving.

Just before serving, turn all the swordfish slices over to make sure they are well covered in oil on both sides and sprinkle them with the chopped fresh parsley. Serve the carpaccio with plenty of crusty bread.

LINGUINE AL CAVIALE ROSSO E NERO

Linguine with Red and Black Caviar

SERVES 6

1 lb linguine, spaghettini, vermicelli, or bavette
salt and freshly ground pepper
5 tablespoons unsalted butter
¼ cup whipping cream, thick plain yogurt or crème fraîche (optional)
1 jar each of red and black caviar (total amount of caviar must be at least 2½ oz)

Bring a large pot of salted water to a boil. Add a large pinch of salt and toss in the pasta. Stir together quickly to prevent sticking, and boil until *al dente* – about 7-9 minutes.

Meanwhile, make the caviar sauce. Melt the butter, without browning it, in a small pan. Add plenty of freshly ground black pepper and the cream or yogurt, if using, and stir quickly to blend it all together.

Drain the pasta and transfer into a warm bowl. Remove the sauce from heat, stir in the caviar, and pour the sauce over the drained pasta. (Do not let the caviar cook or you'll lose its all too elusive flavor. The beauty of this dish is its speed!) Toss together quickly and serve at once.

LINGUINE AL CAVIALE ROSSO E NERO

PASTA

The most widely available and most widely used pasta in Italy is the dry durum wheat variety. Factory made, from just flour and water, it comes in literally hundreds of shapes and sizes and is the staple for Italian cooks in everyday cooking. On special occasions they may turn to fresh pasta, which is actually pasta made with egg and flour. Fresh pasta is sold both dried in packets and soft – in Italy you can buy the latter by weight in a *pastificio*. It is also made at home – for special occasions the rolling pin comes out, the sleeves are rolled up, and love, patience, and sheer energy are all invested in the resulting pasta.

As well as flour and eggs, salt and olive oil can also be added: salt will make the dough stiffer and oil will make it softer. As you become more expert at making pasta, you will come to know which texture you need, depending on what the pasta is to be used for. For instance, cannelloni need to be made from quite soft dough so the tubes can be rolled easily, while the dough for sheets of lasagne should be stiffer; complicated little pasta pockets need extremely flexible dough, whereas with something easy like tagliatelle it does not really matter.

In making fresh pasta, the most useful thing to have besides a pair of strong arms is a good rolling pin – the long Italian ones are the very best for this purpose. And remember that you will need plenty of space to spread out in if you are making a large quantity. Finally, do keep in mind that fresh egg pasta dries out very quickly, and when dry it is brittle and unmanageable. Do *not* leave it on the work top rolled out and ready to use for any longer than you need to before cutting or filling it.

INGREDIENTS FOR PASTA *With the eggs, add salt or olive oil, depending on how flexible you need the pasta to be.*

You will need the following ingredients:

PER PERSON

¾ cup all-purpose flour
1 egg
a pinch of salt (optional)
or
1 teaspoon olive oil (optional)

Put the flour in a pile on the work top and plunge your fist into the middle to make a hole. Break the eggs into the hole and add the salt or olive oil at this point if using. With your fingers begin to knead everything together very thoroughly, gradually working the flour into the eggs until everything is amalgamated. Then with your hands begin to roll and fold the dough over and over again, until it becomes cool and is smooth and elastic.

Once the dough has reached this stage, begin to roll it out. Roll it out as far as possible, fold it in half, then roll it out again. Repeat this over and over until you hear a slapping sound. This means the air is being pressed out from between the layers and the dough is ready to use.

For *tortellini*, first make the meat filling:

FILLS 200 TORTELLINI

3 oz fresh bone marrow
⅓ cup freshly grated Parmesan cheese
2 tablespoons butter
2 oz prosciutto crudo, finely chopped
2 oz mortadella, finely chopped
2 egg yolks
a pinch of salt
a pinch of grated nutmeg

Put the bone marrow into a small bowl and place over a pan of warm water to soften the marrow. Remove the bowl from the heat and mash the marrow to a purée with a fork. Add the cheese, butter, prosciutto, and mortadella. Stir in the egg yolks and season to taste.

For tortellini, add olive oil to the dough, and cut into 1½ inch-squares. In each square, place a very small amount of filling and join two opposite corners to make a triangle. Wrap the triangle around your index finger, folding the two bottom corners in to overlap. Then push the third corner through them to make a rounded pocket shape and push the *tortellino* off with your other hand.

Knead the dough with your fingers until it is smooth and elastic.

Place a tiny amount of meat filling in the center of each square.

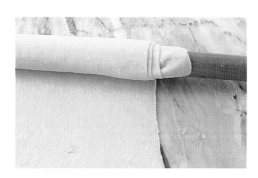

Roll out the dough over and over again – it helps to have a long rolling pin.

Fold in the corners of the squares to make rounded pasta pockets.

TORTELLINI IN BRODO

Pasta Hats in Chicken Broth

SERVES 6

1 medium-sized stewing chicken or a 4½ lb roaster chicken
1 large carrot, chopped coarsely
1 large stalk celery, chopped coarsely
1 large white onion, studded with 1 clove
2 bay leaves
a handful of fresh parsley
a handful of celery leaves
salt and freshly ground pepper
2½ quarts water
¾ lb fresh, ready-made tortellini with a meat filling
freshly grated Parmesan cheese to taste

Put the chicken into a large saucepan with all the vegetables and herbs. Season generously with salt and pepper and cover with the water. Bring to a boil, then cover and simmer about 2 hours or until the chicken is cooked through and the vegetables are soft.

Remove from the heat, and strain the broth into a large china or glass bowl. Cool completely, then refrigerate overnight.

Skim the fat off the surface of the chilled broth and strain the broth again into a large saucepan. Reheat the broth slowly and bring it to a boil. Toss in the tortellini and stir gently so they don't split. Cook about 4-5 minutes, until they are cooked through.

Transfer the soup to a tureen and serve steaming hot with plenty of freshly grated Parmesan cheese offered separately for your guests to add to taste.

SPINACI ALLA GENOVESE

Spinach with Raisins and Pine Nuts

SERVES 8

4½ lb fresh bulk spinach, washed and trimmed
1 stick of butter
⅔ cup raisins, soaked in warm water 10 minutes
1 cup pine nuts
salt

Steam the spinach about 4 minutes or until half cooked. Drain it carefully and squeeze out any remaining water with your hands.

Melt the butter in a large pan, add the spinach, and mix together using 2 forks. Drain the raisins and add them to the spinach, followed by the pine nuts. Mix all together, add salt to taste, and serve at once.

CIPOLLE ARROSTO

Roast Onions

SERVES 8

8 medium-sized, even-shaped red onions
1 egg
⅓ cup freshly grated Parmesan cheese
2 tablespoons brandy
salt and freshly ground pepper
2 tablespoons fresh bread crumbs
2 tablespoons butter
4 tablespoons olive oil

Drop the onions into a pot of boiling water and leave them there about 2 minutes. Remove them with a slotted spoon and peel them quickly. Cut the top and bottom off each one and press out the heart from inside each onion to create a hollow. Chop the hearts finely and put them in a small bowl with the egg. Add the Parmesan cheese, brandy, and salt and pepper to taste. Stir thoroughly. Mix in the bread crumbs. Spoon this mixture into the hollow created inside each onion.

Butter an ovenproof dish and set the stuffed onions in the dish in neat rows. Brush with oil and dot with butter. Cover loosely with foil and bake in a preheated moderately hot oven (375°F) about 45 minutes to 1 hour or until the onions are tender all the way through.

SHELLING PINE NUTS (left) *Pine nuts are extracted from the cones of the stone pine and getting at the kernels can be hard work.*

FARAONA ALLA VERONESE (above), *and served with a slice of fried polenta* (below).

FARAONA ALLA VERONESE

Veronese Guinea Fowl

SERVES 6-8

2 small guinea fowl, cut up
2 tablespoons all-purpose flour
a large pinch of salt
3 tablespoons sunflower oil
¾ cup dry white wine
1¼ cups chicken stock, kept hot
3 green or red sweet peppers
½ lb celery, washed and cut into lengths, or celeriac, peeled and cubed
5 tablespoons Grand Marnier
⅔ cup golden raisins, soaked in warm water 10 minutes

Carefully trim some of the fat off the guinea fowl pieces. Mix the flour and salt together and coat the pieces, shaking off any excess. Heat the oil in a large skillet and fry until golden brown all over. Drain on paper towels and transfer to a flameproof baking dish.

Add the wine and about 2 ladlefuls of the stock to the dish and cook covered on top of the stove for 25 minutes on a low heat. Meanwhile, bring a large pot of water to a boil, toss in the peppers and blanch about 4 minutes. Drain, then cut into 1-inch squares and set aside. Cook the celery or celeriac in boiling salted water until tender; drain.

Warm the Grand Marnier and pour over the guinea fowl, and flame it. Arrange the vegetables around the guinea fowl. Drain the raisins and add them to the dish, with a little more stock to cover the ingredients. Cover and cook in a preheated moderate oven (350°F) 10-12 minutes. Serve hot on a large platter.

IL MONTEBIANCO

The Mont Blanc

SERVES *5-6*

1¾ *lb (about 2 pints) fresh chestnuts*
2 *tablespoons boiling hot milk*
1 *teaspoon vanilla extract*
1¼ *cups confectioners' sugar, sifted*
1 *tablespoon brandy*
1¼ *cups whipping cream (sweetened to taste)*
1 *teaspoon unsweetened cocoa powder*

Put the chestnuts in a saucepan, cover with cold water, and bring to a boil. Cook until tender. Peel them quickly while still hot so that the inner brown skin comes away easily. Push the still hot chestnuts through a vegetable mill on a very fine setting. Mix the resulting purée *lightly* with a fork.

Stir the milk, vanilla extract, sugar, and brandy together and stir this *lightly* into the chestnut purée. Push this mixture through a vegetable mill on the finest setting, letting it fall onto a platter in a mountain shape. Whip the cream. Cover the mountain *lightly* with the cream, dust with cocoa powder around the base, and serve at once, or chill until required.

You are aiming for lightness of texture, so be careful how you handle these ingredients! An alternative is to cover the dish onto which you will build the cake with a layer of crushed meringues. For this quantity, use about 5 fist-sized meringues, broken into pieces.

IL MONTEBIANCO (left), PANFORTE (right)

CANDIED FRUITS (right) *Candied fruits and peel are used in many Christmas specialties.*

PANFORTE

Sienese Sweetmeat

For authenticity, candied popone should be used in this sweetmeat, but if you can't get hold of it, use candied peel.

MAKES ONE 8–INCH CAKE

1⅓ cups shelled almonds
¾ cup shelled walnuts
2 cups all-purpose flour
2 cups finely chopped candied peel
a pinch each of ground cinnamon, ground coriander, ground cloves, and grated nutmeg
1½ cups sugar
rice paper
extra 2 teaspoons ground cinnamon

Blanch the almonds and the walnuts separately in boiling water. Remove the skins, then chop or grind the nuts separately into a fine powder.

Set aside about 3 tablespoons of flour. Mix the remaining flour with the chopped candied peel. Stir in the chopped almonds, then the chopped walnuts and then the spices.

Put the sugar in a very small heavy-bottomed saucepan with just enough water to dampen it. Heat until you achieve a "rubbery" texture, not a syrup. Mix this into the rest of the ingredients and stir thoroughly.

Line an 8–inch layer cake pan with rice paper. Spread the nut mixture out well in the pan. Sprinkle over the reserved flour mixed with the 2 teaspoons of cinnamon. Bake in a preheated moderately hot oven (375°F) about 30 minutes. Shake off the loose flour and cinnamon from the top, and cool the cake before serving. (It will remain flat and unrisen.)

ACKNOWLEDGMENTS

Valentina Harris and Conran Octopus would like to thank the following people for their help:
Giulia dell'Amico, Beppino and Andreina de Battisti, Eleonora Carpi, Eleonora Consoli (Catania), Katia Fongoli, Aldo di Maria (Palermo), Ferruccio Nobile Migliore, Conte and Contessa Notabartolo (Catania), Maria-Teresa Olcese (Milano), Cristina Pagani (Milano), Gerardo and Cetty Rossano (Palermo), Salvatore Rubino (Palermo), Howard, Linda, Lucia and Benedetta Scott and friends, Nicholas and Daniel.

For front jacket photography styling: Jane Newdick
For front jacket photography art direction: Georgina Rhodes